Philip Allan
Publishers

A-Level

Exam
Success
Guide

Geography
Essays

Dick Knowles

Titles available

A-Level

Geography: Essays

Biology: Essays

British History, 1815–1951

Business Studies: Essays

Chemistry: Multiple Choice

Chemistry: Structured Questions & Essays

Computing

Economics: Data Response

Economics: Essays

Economics: Multiple Choice

English: Practical Criticism

European History, 1789–1945

French

History: Europe of the Dictators, 1914–1945

Law: General Principles

Media Studies

Physics: Structured Questions & Multiple Choice

Politics: Essays

Pure Mathematics

Religious Studies: The New Testament — The Gospels

Religious Studies: The Philosophy of Religion

Sociology: Essays

Philip Allan Publishers Limited
Market Place
Deddington
Oxfordshire OX15 0SE

Telephone: 01869 338652

Formerly published by Richard Ball Publishing
Revised 1998

ISBN 0 86003 334 1

This is a revised edition of *A-Level Geography: Essays* published by Richard Ball Publishing in 1995.

Typeset by Alden Bookset, Oxford and printed by Information Press, Eynsham, Oxford

Contents

Contents

Introduction

This Exam Success Guide contains a wide selection of questions similar to those used in A-level geography examination papers. For each question, a full answer has been prepared to demonstrate the type of response which should attract high marks from the examiner. The questions cover both physical and human geography, together with the important area of overlap and interaction between these two traditional branches of the subject which increasingly forms an applied focus for geographical and environmental studies.

The Guide also contains a number of unique and helpful features. Each answer is prefaced with a section entitled *Tackling the Question* which provides useful hints on the style of the question and the importance of the topic, as well as pointing out any problems or 'traps' you may encounter in planning and preparing your answer. *Guidance Notes* alongside the answer itself provide step-by-step comments on the style and content of the answer and show the thought processes and decision making that go into answer planning and essay writing. In addition, there are *General Comments* at the end of each answer. These draw attention to any special features of either the question or the answer itself. *Related Questions* then follow. These cover the same or closely related topics, but are presented in different styles and formats. A few apply the same question format to unrelated topics.

The Guide aims to cover all the different types of question format you might encounter at A-level, with the exception of data-response questions. Thus there are traditional, formal essay titles which offer little or no guidance to what is expected in the answer. There are part-questions with numbered subsections, and part-questions with designated allocations of marks. There are questions which require descriptions of fieldwork and practical experience, and others which require comments on various techniques of geographical analysis. There are 'closed questions', which require reference to specific named regions and case studies, and 'open questions' which allow reference to any area or example that you might have studied on a particular topic. You should make yourself familiar with all these types of question.

This Guide does *not* contain 'model' answers. It would be presumptuous to suggest that there is a single 'right' answer to any of these questions against which other answers should be compared. These essays represent my own thoughts and responses to a series of questions which are similar to those you will encounter in your A-level examination. They will evoke different responses from you, according to your background, experience and knowledge. In A-level geography there is certainly no single correct answer to an essay question. You could equally well argue an opposite case to many of the questions included here; provided you did it logically and with skill and backed it up with factual information and examples, you would still satisfy the examiner.

What the answers in this Guide do provide are examples of good practice. They illustrate the various ingredients expected in a good A-level answer. They have been carefully planned and display an ordered sequence of ideas and argument. Each essay has an introduction, in which terms are usually defined and the parameters of the answer established, and a conclusion, which serves as a summary or recapitulation of key facts and ideas, or as an evaluation of opposing arguments. (New factual material should not be introduced in the concluding paragraph.) The main body of each essay is divided into paragraphs, each of which deals with a single major theme. It should be possible to extract a single paragraph from any well-written essay, read it out of context and still be able to identify its essential theme. Avoid paragraphs which are just depositories for a jumble of disconnected facts and ideas. Restrict yourself to one clearly defined theme per paragraph.

Exam questions always contain what might be described as a 'task word'. This determines what is required in the answer. You will earn few marks for a descriptive answer when the question asks you to evaluate, or if you make a comparison when the question asks you to contrast two features. It is essential that you know exactly what each 'task word' requires, so make sure you understand the exact requirements of each of the following: compare, contrast, criticise, define, describe, discuss, evaluate, illustrate, interpret, justify, outline, review, summarise, and trace.

The best answers in A-level geography display a balanced combination of factual, descriptive material on the one hand, and more abstract, conceptual argument and discussion on the other. Answers should not be dominated by either approach at the expense of the other. When geographical ideas and concepts are introduced they should be backed up by facts, figures and well-chosen examples. This is where solid revision and careful exam preparation are essential. You must have an extensive store of geographical information from which you can shape your answers. It is surprising how many examples and how much information can be introduced into a single essay answer. Wide reading and careful note-taking are essential to sound exam preparation. Be aware of current social and economic trends, and keep your information as up-to-date as possible by reading magazines and journals such as the *Geography Review*.

The answers in this Guide should not be memorised with the intention of reproducing them in the examination. Nor should they be seen as a substitute for the wide reading which is essential in geography. On the other hand, the answers present concise, factual summaries of many key A-level topics and will prove useful if re-read as part of your revision programme.

All statistical information in the Guide is as up-to-date as possible. Statistical data related to population, settlement sizes, economic production, etc., have been derived from the latest available editions of the *UN Demographic Yearbook*, the *UN Statistical Yearbook*, the *Annual Abstract of Statistics* for the UK, and the 1991 *UK Census Report*. As always there is a lag between the date of publication and the date to which the statistics relate.

Question 1

Explain what is measured on the flood hydrograph and outline the factors which affect its form.

Tackling the question

Questions on the flood hydrograph frequently appear in the section of the A-level examination covering geomorphology. The reason is obvious. Any discussion of the flood hydrograph requires a clear understanding of the various factors which affect both the timing and volume of fluvial discharge in any river basin. You need to understand the influence of basin size and shape, relief, geology, soils, vegetation as well as human influences on infiltration, overland flow and other aspects of basin hydrology. For the examiner, a single question on the flood hydrograph is a convenient means of testing your understanding of a wide variety of hydrological relationships.

This particular question is in two parts. The first part requires that you explain what is measured on the flood hydrograph, while the second part requires a description of the various factors which affect its form. You could, therefore, divide the answer into two large and distinct sections, but such a plan would almost certainly involve repetition. Alternatively, you could deal with the two sections simultaneously: you could describe each aspect of the flood hydrograph in turn, and at the same time deal with the factors influencing each aspect of the graph. If the two sections of the question had been designated (a) and (b) in the examination question, there might have been a stronger case for organising the answer as two clearly separated situations.

Answer

A flood hydrograph is a form of graph on which river discharge during a storm or **runoff event** is plotted against time. Discharge (Q) is defined as the volume of flow passing through a cross-section of a river during a given period of time, and is usually measured in m^3/sec. Thus, the flood hydrograph provides a continuous picture of the timing of the final, or runoff, stage of the hydrological cycle as recorded for the basin draining through the monitoring site. For this reason, it is not surprising that the reaction of any river to a runoff event, as revealed by the size, shape and peak value of this response graph, reflects many aspects of basin hydrology.

Guidance notes

A definition and brief description of the flood hydrograph serves as an introduction. Essay answers should always have an introductory paragraph, but keep it short and concise.

A diagram of the flood hydrograph is considered essential. Under exam conditions you might not be able to produce something as 'finished' as this, but key diagrams should be memorised and practised as part of your revision. Take coloured pens into the exam room for drawing diagrams and sketch-maps.

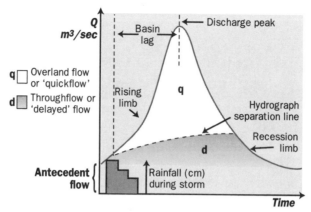

Figure 1 Features of the flood hydrograph

This and the following six paragraphs constitute the main body of the answer. One aspect of the flood hydrograph is dealt with in each paragraph, together with some discussion of the factors affecting each aspect.

Each of the flood hydrograph features identified on Figure 1 has particular hydrological significance. For instance, consider **hydrograph size** as represented by the area under the graph. Generally speaking, the higher the amount of rainfall, the greater will be the discharge value for a given basin. Similarly, for two basins experiencing the same storm, the larger their basin size, the greater will be the discharge recorded on the flood hydrograph. The **discharge peak** is generally higher in large basins than in small basins. However, the timing of the runoff generated is also important. Other things being equal, in steep catchments with low infiltration rates, the response of the catchment will be 'flashy' (i.e. the timing will be fast) and the peaks higher than those in relatively flat catchments of the same size in which high infiltration rates and delayed throughflow predominate.

Basin lag is the time interval between peak rainfall intensity and the **discharge peak**, and at a large scale is influenced by basin shape and basin steepness or gradient. Figure 2 shows how basins of the same size, which are likely to generate hydrographs with the same total area under the graph, may have different basin lags. This is because the long, thin basin (a) delivers runoff volumes over a much longer period at the measuring point than the broader basin (b), in which all the

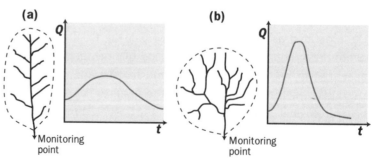

Figure 2 Basins of the same size, with the same rainfall, vary in response due to shape

tributaries deliver water to the monitoring point at much the same time. In response to these differences in the timing of the runoff delivery, the height of the discharge peak is obviously altered too.

Because basin shape is closely related to stream order and bifurcation ratios, these two factors are also thought to exert control over hydrograph shape. It is also the case that the higher velocities associated with steep terrain speed up travel time in a basin, thereby reducing lag time and increasing peak size and **rising limb** steepness. In other words, many of the physical characteristics of a drainage basin affect runoff response.

However, both basin lag and rising limb steepness are related to infiltration. Since **overland flow** or **quickflow** (i.e. rain in excess of infiltration) arrive at the monitoring point rapidly in comparison with **throughflow** or **delayed flow,** two basins which were identical in their permanent controls but differed in their peak shape could be assumed to differ in terms of the route taken by the rainfall (i.e. variations in the ratio of delayed flow through the ground to overland flow over the surface). Rates of infiltration can be drastically affected by land use changes; these in turn will alter the hydrograph response for the reasons described above.

The shape of the **recession limb**, or graph of receding flow, indicates the rate of groundwater depletion caused by delayed flow after every rainfall event. This curve yields information about the geological composition and behaviour of local aquifers. Geology is very important in hydrology because of its influence on soils and infiltration characteristics of the catchment, as well this direct control on the recession behaviour of the flood.

Antecedent flow is the pre-existing value of discharge in the river before the flood commences, and suggests the level of delayed flow in the catchment in percentage terms. Thus, it has a high value in catchments with large amounts of infiltration. When rainfall events are distinct temporally, an assumption is made that the antecedent flow is entirely made up of delayed flow. However, although delayed flow contributing to channel flow will increase during a storm, it rarely explains the peak, since overland flow in excess of infiltration enters the channel in increasing amounts as time goes on. Thus, it is possible to identify a **hydrograph separation line** which distinguishes the delayed flow from the overland or quickflow on the hydrograph.

The **ratio of quickflow to delayed flow** can be calculated right through the storm once the hydrograph has been separated. This ratio tends to be high in areas with low infiltration rates experiencing high-intensity rain. This is often the case in semi-arid areas. The hydrograph in Figure 3(a) illustrates this situation. On the other hand, where the ratio of quickflow to delayed flow is low, this indicates an environment dominated by throughflow, with good infiltration rates and little overland flow. This is typical of humid areas with good, deep soils and abundant vegetation. Figure 3(b) illustrates this situation. More than any other hydrograph characteristic, the ratio between quickflow and delayed flow tends to be climatically controlled.

These diagrams are not essential. The same information could be conveyed in two or three sentences. As you approach the end of an answer, check that you are still writing to schedule. If time is short, don't bother with the diagrams. Include them only if you have time to spare.

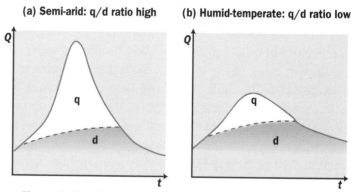

(a) Semi-arid: q/d ratio high   **(b) Humid-temperate: q/d ratio low**

Figure 3 Two identical basins react differently in differing climatic areas

The concluding paragraph is of the 'summary-type'. Key points from the answer are briefly reiterated. Not very original, but quite acceptable.

In conclusion, it can be seen that there are both **permanent controls** and **transient controls** on flood hydrograph shape and size. The permanent controls are those of basin size, shape, steepness, geology, vegetation and soils. The transient controls are those to do with climatic variability, such as rainfall intensity, frequency, amount and type. Transient controls also include various human influences such as changes to the infiltration properties of watershed surfaces brought about by processes such as deforestation and urbanisation.

General comments

If your examination includes data-response questions, then you should be prepared for questions on the flood hydrograph in that section of the exam. You might be presented with graphs for different catchments and be asked to make explanatory comparisons. Alternatively, you might be required to take measurements of discharge or lag times from a specimen hydrograph. In many ways it is easier for the examiner to test your understanding of the flood hydrograph with a data-response question rather than a formal essay question. A data-response question is probably the safest bet.

Related questions

1 Identify and comment on the conditions which can cause river floods in the United Kingdom.

2 Examine ways in which human activity can modify patterns of river discharge.

3 With reference to any one drainage basin, discuss the factors which influence temporal variations in discharge.

Explain the meaning of each of the following terms used in drainage basin analysis and comment on any relationships that exist between them: (a) catchment area; (b) stream order; (c) stream number; (d) drainage density; (e) bifurcation ratio.

Tackling the question

This question is concerned with drainage basin analysis; specifically, the techniques of fluvial morphometry, or quantitative analysis. The style of question is unusual for an A-level examination, but not unknown. You are presented with five key terms employed in drainage basin analysis, and simply asked to 'explain the meaning' of each. Faced with this particular question format, you need to make some quick decisions.

Does each part of the question carry equal weight and should the answers be of roughly equal length? Since there is no allocation of marks in the question, the answer is 'yes' to both questions. Roughly how long can be spent on each section? You will need to make that calculation for your own particular exam, but you will probably have no more than seven or eight minutes for each section. In other words, you will probably have time for just one or two paragraphs on each section. And exactly what is the examiner looking for in these answers? 'Explain the meaning' is not the same as 'define'. What is needed is a definition of each term together with some brief elaboration and comment. There is the additional task of commenting on any relationships between the various terms. This is best done, where appropriate, in each section rather than as a separate section at the end of the answer.

Answer

(a) Catchment area

This is a concise, compact paragraph with a well-chosen example to illustrate catchment hierarchies.

The term **catchment area** refers to the area from which a river receives water by way of rainfall, surface drainage or percolation. It is the collecting ground for the water supply of a river or stream. The term catchment area is synonymous with a number of other terms, including drainage basin, catchment basin and gathering ground. The boundary of a catchment area is known as a watershed or divide. The boundary separates the waters flowing into two adjacent drainage basins. Within a single large catchment area, it is possible to identify a series of lower order catchment areas. For example, the whole of the Mississippi Basin forms a single vast catchment area covering more than half the area of the USA but, within it, there are the secondary catchment areas of major rivers such as the Missouri, Arkansas, Ohio and Tennessee. Those rivers in turn are fed by tributaries also with clearly definable catchment areas. In other words, a 'nested' hierarchy of catchment areas can usually be identified within large drainage basins.

The pattern of drainage within a catchment area may be described by a series of subjective, impressionistic terms, such as dendritic, semi-dendritic, trellised, rectangular, parallel, radial and so on. These terms, which have been described as 'naively pictorial', lack objectivity and precision, and in recent years have been largely replaced by quantitative techniques of drainage basin analysis.

(b) Stream order

The term **fluvial morphometry** is used to describe the quantitative investigation of the geometric properties of rivers and their basins. The great advantage of measurement and quantification lies in the precision that is gained. Different river basins can be precisely compared, and correlations can be undertaken between different variables affecting drainage patterns. Techniques of fluvial morphometry were first devised by R.E. Horton in the 1940s and later developed by A.N. Strahler, S.A. Schumm and others.

These are some early workers in the field of fluvial morphometry. Bonus marks if you are familiar with them and mention their names.

A basic aim in fluvial morphometry is to establish a hierarchy of streams ranked according to order. Various methods of **stream ordering** have been devised, but that of A.N. Strahler remains the most widely used.

According to Strahler's method, streams at the head of a drainage system (fingertip streams) are designated as first-order streams; two first-order streams join to form a second-order stream; two second-order streams join to form a third-order stream, and so on. It takes at least two streams of a given order to form a stream of the next-highest order. If a lower-order stream (say, first-order) joins a higher-order stream (say, third-order), the order of the latter remains unchanged. A confluence, where a change of order occurs, is called a **promotion point**.

The system of stream ordering is described in the text. The inclusion of the diagram is, therefore, something of a luxury, intended simply to clarify the text. If time is short, leave it out.

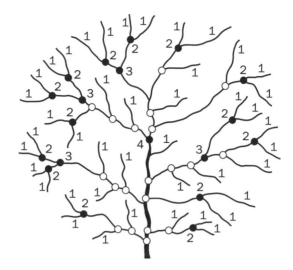

● Promotion point where next order begins

○ Non-promotion point. No change of order

Figure 1 Stream ordering according to A.N. Strahler

(c) Stream number

The term **stream number** describes the number of streams in each order within a given drainage basin. Using the hypothetical example in Figure 1, the following information can be tabulated for stream orders and stream numbers.

Stream order	Stream number
1	43
2	14
3	4
4	1

The Law of Stream Numbers is important in this context. It provides material for the second part of the question on relationships between the various terms and concepts. It is not essential to mention the Law of Stream Lengths or the Law of Basin Areas, especially if time is short.

R.E. Horton noted that an orderly arrangement of streams of different orders existed in most drainage basins, and proposed a series of **Laws of Drainage Composition**. He noted, for example, that the stream numbers of different orders decreased in a regular manner with the increase in stream order. If stream orders are plotted against the logarithm of stream numbers for each order, a straight-line relationship emerges. This regularity is known as the **Law of Stream Numbers**. A relationship also exists between stream order and the mean length of streams. The mean length of streams of each progressively higher order increases in a regular manner. This is the **Law of Stream Lengths**. Conversely, the area drained by streams of each progressively higher order decreases in a regular manner. This is the **Law of Basin Areas**.

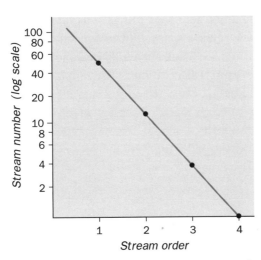

Figure 2 The relationship between stream orders
and stream numbers

Again, the graph is here to simply clarify the written explanation. You may feel that it is not necessary to include the graph, and that the written explanation of the Law of Stream Numbers is perfectly clear without any illustration.

(d) Drainage density

Drainage density represents another approach to the quantitative analysis of drainage basins. Drainage density is simply a measure of the average length of river channel per unit area of the drainage basin.

$$\text{Drainage density} = \frac{\text{Total stream length}}{\text{Total area of basin}}$$

Values for drainage density vary widely from basin to basin. In the UK, most drainage densities lie within the range of 2–4 km/km^2, although on highly permeable surfaces, such as areas of mountain limestone, values may fall to less than 1 km/km^2. In the USA, values as high as 700 km/km^2 have been recorded in areas of highly dissected 'badlands' topography. Drainage density is affected by many variables including geology, structure, relief, soils, precipitation and vegetation characteristics.

Some examples are useful to show the range of values that might be expected.

(e) Bifurcation ratio

The **bifurcation ratio** of any drainage system, or part of a drainage system, is the ratio between the number of streams of one order and the number of streams of the next-highest order.

$$\text{Bifurcation ratio} = \frac{\text{Number of first-order streams}}{\text{Number of second-order streams}}$$

Question 2

With this type of part-question it is not necessary to write a conclusion or to sum up the whole answer.

The bifurcation ratios for the various orders of streams can be averaged to give a mean bifurcation ratio for the drainage basin as a whole, although such a figure is not particularly informative or revealing. Bifurcation ratios usually range from 3.0 to 5.0. The bifurcation ratio provides a quantitative expression of the relative importance of the parts or orders of a drainage network, unlike the drainage density measurement which is simply concerned with the average or overall density of the network as a whole.

General comments

With part-questions, such as this, you don't have to spend time on or worry about an essay plan. The question also requires largely factual material. You don't have to think about arguments and counter-arguments, and produce a balanced evaluation of different positions. This type of question is really a test of factual recall. It requires a lot of information which has to be assembled and organised very quickly under exam conditions. Speed is of the essence. You can afford to spend no more than a few minutes on each of the five sections. If you find yourself over-running your allocated time for one section, then quickly draw it to a close. You will score more marks from five modest answers than from two or three in great detail and the others unfinished.

Related questions

1   In what ways can the techniques of fluvial morphometry aid our understanding of the processes operating in drainage basins?

2   Justify the use of statistical techniques in the study of drainage basins.

3   Describe how you would make a statistical comparison of the patterns of drainage in two small river catchments.

Question 3

Describe the project organisation and the field techniques which you might employ in a survey of *either* (a) the processes operating along a short section of a small meandering stream, *or* (b) the distribution of plant species in a small area of chalk downland.

Tackling the question

This type of question is designed to test and confirm that you have actually participated in some practical fieldwork as part of your preparation for the A-level geography examination. It requires a description of the organisation and field techniques used in studies of either stream channel characteristics and discharge or plant species distribution. Such descriptions are not easy to write. You need to recall and include the logistical decisions which were made as part of the project planning, as well as the instrumentation and techniques of measurement employed. Notice that the question does not ask about data analysis, interpretation or presentation. Don't get drawn into those aspects of fieldwork.

Answer

Guidance notes

(a) Survey of processes operating along a short section of a small meandering stream

The organisation of a survey of fluvial processes operating along a short section of a small meandering stream will be determined by practical and logistical considerations such as the size of the survey team, the time available for data collection and analysis, and the type of field equipment and laboratory facilities available. The following description relates to a very basic type of survey which might be undertaken with relatively limited time and means available. Most of the techniques described will yield adequate results and are relatively easy to undertake in the field. Other more complex and sophisticated techniques, some involving continuous instrumentation, are used by professional hydrologists and fluvial geomorphologists.

Although it should rapidly become evident which part of the question you have answered, nevertheless it is good practice to identify your choice. Make the examiner's life as easy as possible.

This paragraph deals with some of the considerations which influence the choice of project location.

The selection of a suitable channel section for survey is a first consideration. Possibilities might be identified from large-scale topographical maps such as the Ordnance Survey 1:10 000 series. The aim is to locate a typical, representative section. The survey site should be relatively uniform in character and should be free from any major obstructions — large boulders, bridges, fallen trees, etc. — which might distort flow patterns. It should not be located immediately downstream of a tributary confluence, and should be free of waterfalls, rapids or constrictions. It should include a clearly developed sequence of pools and riffles which are central to any study of stream meanders.

This paragraph provides the context for the answer. It briefly reviews some of the variables involved in stream discharge and channel form. It leads logically to a consideration of what data might be collected. The diagrams aid and support the description of this material, but if you are short of time they are not essential to the answer.

Pools are sections of deeper water usually found on the outside of meander bends; **riffles** are sections of shallow water (shoals) usually found between meander loops (see Figure 1a). The movement of water in river channels adopts what are described as helical or helicoidal spirals. These occur along the channel at regular intervals and tend to produce a repeating sequence of bedforms. Although the mechanics of stream flow are highly complex and not fully understood, it is thought that when the spirals have a downward directed component in the centre of the channel, pools form. Conversely, where a 'lift' occurs in the centre of the channel, riffles form. These differences tend to cause erosion during highflow in the pools, after which material is deposited onto the riffles (see Figures 1b and c). As a result there is an oversteepening of riffle slopes compared with pool slopes. This in turn means that velocities are greater on riffles than on pools. This is just one example of the relationships that exist between stream discharge (Q), channel width (W), channel depth (D) and stream velocity (V). Those relationships can be summarised by the basic equation for hydraulic geometry:

$$Q = W \times D \times V$$

Other relationships that exist are those between stream load (type, size, calibre, etc.) and discharge, velocity and channel processes of erosion, transportation and deposition.

(a) Pool and riffle seqence on a meandering stream

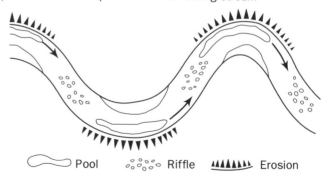

Pool   Riffle   Erosion

(b) Convergent and divergent flow in plan

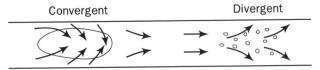

Convergent   Divergent

(c) Convergent and divergent flow in section

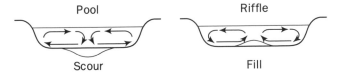

Pool   Riffle

Scour   Fill

(d) Surface flow vectors on a meander bend

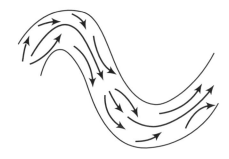

Figure 1

From these comments, it is clear that a field study of a section of meandering stream might concentrate on any one of a number of hydraulic relationships. It might consider, for example, the relationships between channel characteristics and stream velocity for a given level of discharge. In theory, it might involve a **time element** whereby a comparison is made between processes operating under high-water and low-water conditions, or at different seasons of the year. However, temporal studies are difficult to organise, and a small-scale study concentrating on spatial variations is more likely to be successful. This would involve the recording of data at 10 to 20 **sampling points** along the stream. These sampling points might be chosen randomly or selected to coincide with pools and riffles. At each sampling point a set of basic data would then be collected. Typically, this might include measurements of discharge, velocity, channel width and depth, transported load and stream bed deposits. The techniques for collecting these data are described below.

Stream discharge is 'the volume of water passing a given point on the river bank over a given time'. Volume is normally expressed in cubic metres per second (cumecs) or sometimes in litres per second. In order to calculate discharge, two pieces of information are required: stream velocity and the cross-sectional area of the stream channel. Measurement of

This paragraph describes the techniques of measuring discharge. This is a product of velocity and channel shape and size.

velocity can be undertaken in one of two ways: either by timing the passage of floats along measured section (10–30 m), or by using a velocity-meter (current-meter). The latter is simply a propeller device attached to a rev-counter. Using floats, allowance has to be made for the fact that surface flow is faster than subsurface flow (multiply surface readings by 0.85), and also the fact that bankside flow is slower than central-channel flow (take the average of several surface readings). Velocity (m/sec) is obtained by dividing distance (m) by time (secs). A **cross-sectional area** of the channel can be obtained by using a measuring tape for the width and a measuring pole to probe the depth of the stream at regular intervals (every 50 cm or every metre) across the channel. These results can be transferred to graph paper, and the cross-sectional area calculated from the scale drawing. Finally, cross-sectional area (m^2) can be multiplied by velocity (m/sec) to give discharge (cumecs).

The sediment transported by any river is referred to as its **load**. This load is of four types; namely, bed-load (stones and pebbles which are rolled along the river-bed), saltation load (smaller material which moves downstream by being 'bounced' off the river-bed), suspended load (fine sand and silt carried by turbulent eddies in the water), and solution load (dissolved minerals in the water). The load carried by any river or stream is difficult to measure accurately. Many of the techniques involved require specialised equipment and laboratory analysis of sediment yield. Some of the techniques for measuring different types of load are identified below.

Measurement of bed-load involves the use of a **bed-load trap**. This is a wooden or metal box which is inserted into a trench dug into the stream bed. After a given period of time (days or weeks) the trap is removed so that its contents can be weighed and analysed. Saltation load and suspended load are also difficult to measure. One method involves the use of a **sediment sampler**. This is essentially a type of bottle which is lowered from the water surface down to the bed of the stream and back to the surface again. The volume of the water sample is measured and recorded. In a laboratory the sediment-laden water is filtered through a filter paper of known dry weight. The filter paper plus sediment is dried in an oven before being weighed. It is then possible to calculate the concentration of sediment. This is normally expressed as milligrams per litre (mg/l) or parts per million (ppm). If stream discharge was measured at the same time as the sediment sampling, then it is possible to calculate the total suspended sediment load as grams per second passing a point on the bank.

Solution load can be measured by a **conductivity meter**. This is a meter attached to a probe with two electrodes. When inserted into a stream this measures the electrical conductivity

Measurement of load is much more difficult. The paragraphs which follow describe the instruments and techniques of measurement available.

of the water. The greater the amount of dissolved minerals, the greater the conductivity. In this way it is possible to measure the concentration of solutes (dissolved minerals) in the water. This is largely determined by the geology of the catchment area and its susceptibility to chemical weathering, as well as the relative contributions of ground water, overland flow and throughflow to the stream discharge. However, neither suspended load nor the solution load are likely to vary much through a short section of river.

Given the problems and limitations of measuring stream load, another approach is to consider **stream competence**. This is the strength or efficiency of a stream as indicated by the largest pebble or particle being moved as bed-load. A wide range of sediment sizes is present on the bed of most rivers, but at low flow only the finest grains are moved. At higher flows and velocities, large material may be moved. In other words, stream competence varies in response to changes in discharge. Marked pebbles of different sizes can be introduced into a stream, and the distance travelled by pebbles of different sizes can be measured and recorded.

Stream bed deposits can also be analysed by washing a sample of 100 grams of sediment through a nest of sieves with graduated mesh sizes and weighing the amount retained at each size level. In this way the mean sediment size can be compared for pools and riffles. Normally, pools are floored with relatively fine material (sand and silt), while riffles have a cover of coarser sediment (stones and pebbles). By concentrating on bed-load and bed deposits, the survey places emphasis on channel morphology; that is to say, the **results** of fluvial processes, rather than the **processes** themselves.

Some simpler, alternative techniques are described here. They are more likely to be the ones with which you are familiar.

L.B. Leopold and T. Maddock (1953) were among the first to recognise the existence of causal relationships between fluvial processes and channel morphology. Later, W.B. Langbein (1964) suggested that river channels possess five degrees of freedom, and are able to adjust to changing discharge by modifying their bed roughness, gradient, width, depth and planform in order to restore a state of quasi-equilibrium. Data derived from field surveys of river meanders can allow the quantification and testing of some of the processes involved in those adjustments to the hydraulic geometry of the stream. 'Field surveys provide valuable data describing the characteristics of the channel pattern, particularly when integrated with measurements of cross-sectional form, sediment type and distribution, and flow pattern. Field surveys direct attention towards the inter-relationships between the different attributes of channel form.' (G.E. Petts)

Comments on the importance of field studies serve as a conclusion to the essay. Although rather late in the essay, the names of some key researchers in the field are also mentioned.

It may not be possible to memorise and include very long quotations, but short quotations are equally valuable where relevant.

General Comments

Unless you have actually been involved in a group project or carried out an individual study of stream meanders or the distribution of plants on chalk downland, this type of question is best left alone. Even if you feel well informed about the mechanics of meander development based on textbook study, that doesn't necessarily mean that you could produce a good answer to this question. It is essential that you demonstrate 'hands-on', practical experience.

Related questions

1 Describe how you might set up a field experiment to demonstrate relationships between stream velocity and transported load.

2 Describe how you would identify and measure the changes taking place along a section of shingle beach crossed by groynes.

3 Describe how you would set up an experiment to monitor the regeneration of an area of heathland vegetation following its destruction by burning.

Question 4

(a) Explain what is meant by the term 'periglaciation'.

(b) Describe the landscape features which result from periglacial processes.

Tackling the question

This is a two-part question, but no allocation of marks is indicated for the two components. In the absence of this information, you should always assume that the two parts carry equal marks. However, on the face of it, the two parts appear to be rather unequal in their demands. Part (a) could be interpreted as simply requiring a definition of the term 'periglaciation'. That is done in the first paragraph. Clearly, something more must be required. Somehow, the simple definition must be expanded. Thus, the first part of the answer includes some discussion of the differences between Icelandic and Siberian periglacial regimes, as well as the contrasts between continuous and discontinuous permafrost. In that way, the two sections of the answer assume roughly equal length and weight. All of this indicates the importance of careful essay planning before you start composing the answer.

Part (b) is relatively easy. The examiners will almost certainly have a long checklist of 'landscape features', from pingos to polygons, which might be included in the answer. Each one that you identify and describe will earn marks. Try to include as many as possible. Solid revision is the key to success with this type of question.

Answer

Guidance notes

(a) The term 'periglacial' was first introduced by W.V. Lozinski in 1909 to describe 'areas adjacent to the borders of the Pleistocene ice-sheets, the climatic characteristics of those areas, and, by extension, the phenomena induced by that particular type of environment'. Put very simply, the adjective 'periglacial' describes areas lying adjacent to a former or contemporary ice-sheet, together with their climatic and landform characteristics. **Periglaciation** refers to the geomorphological processes which operate in those areas lying adjacent to glaciers and ice-sheets.

Periglacial areas are found in high latitudes or at high altitudes. Located close to areas of permanent snow and ice,

This first paragraph consists of a short, concise definition.

Two different types of periglacial regime are introduced here. Notice how a good selection of type-areas is worked into each paragraph.

Another distinction is introduced here; namely, that between continuous and discontinuous permafrost. The point is supported by some useful factual detail.

they experience temperatures well below freezing in winter, and a brief summer period when temperatures may rise above freezing. The term 'periglacial' literally means 'peripheral to glaciers', but is usually applied in a wider sense to all areas in which frost action involving freezing of the ground is the dominant geomorphological process. Some parts of the world experience a climatic regime in which temperature constantly fluctuates above and below the 0°C level. Such areas include Southern Alaska, parts of Iceland, Northern Scandinavia and South Georgia in the South Atlantic. This type of periglacial climate is sometimes referred to as **Icelandic**. Other parts of the world experience perennial freezing of the ground. Winter conditions are so intensely cold and the ground so deeply frozen that even the summer warmth fails to thaw it out. The result is permafrost or permanently frozen ground. This occurs in Northern Alaska, Northern Canada, Greenland and Siberia. This type of periglacial climate is described as **Siberian**.

Normally, two belts of **permafrost** are identified: a zone of **continuous permafrost** at the highest latitudes and altitudes; and a zone of **discontinuous permafrost** at lower latitudes and altitudes. It has been estimated that almost 25% of the earth's land surface is underlain by continuous or discontinuous permafrost, so that its extent and importance should not be under-estimated. In the continuous permafrost zone, permafrost is present at all localities, while in the discontinuous permafrost zone, patches of deeply frozen ground are separated by unfrozen areas. The division between the two zones corresponds roughly with the July 10°C isotherm. Permafrost is known to extend to depths of 1,500 m below the surface in Northern Siberia and depths of about 100 m in Northern Canada. Above the

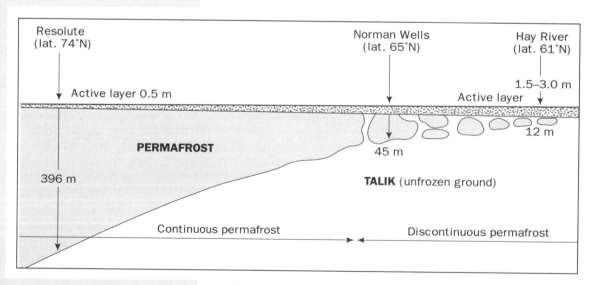

Figure 1 A longitudinal transect through part of the permafrost zones in Northern Canada (after A. Goudie)

permafrost layer, there is usually a thin layer of soil or peat which thaws out in summer. This zone, known as the **active layer**, varies in thickness from as little as 15 cm to a maximum of about 5 m in places.

Obviously, the Icelandic and Siberian types of periglacial regime merge gradually with one another. Nevertheless, the distinction is a useful one since particular landforms are associated with each type of climatic environment. For example, features such as ice-wedge polygons can only form in permafrost, while stone-sorted patterns require repeated freeze–thaw cycles. The various landforms which develop under the two types of periglacial conditions will be explained next.

(b) The ground ice in permafrost regions occurs in many forms. Sometimes it takes the form of massive ice or block ice, but very often occurs as **ice wedges**, about one metre wide at the surface. Intense winter cold may cause the ground to crack into roughly polygonal networks (**unsorted polygons**). These cracks become progressively wider as each summer they are filled with moisture which later freezes and prevents the crack from closing. Another form of ground ice is described by the term **pingo**. This is a large ice mound, 10–60 m in height and up to 300 m in diameter. Pingos form when subterranean water is forced towards the surface, usually by artesian pressure. The water freezes just above the permafrost in the active layer to form a lens-shaped ice mass which in turn causes the overlying sediment to become domed upwards to form a distinctive surface feature. Examples are common in the tundra region of Northern Canada. Subsequent melting of the ice produces a pingo mound, a roughly-circular rampart enclosing a central depression which is usually waterfilled and often lined with peat.

When permafrost melts, either as a result of climatic change or because of the disturbance of the ground by human activity, it does so in a seemingly chaotic way. Enclosed hollows, small lakes, hummocks and ridges are all typical landscape results of

In the second part of the answer the emphasis is on the description of what are essentially minor landscape features. You are asked to 'describe', so don't get diverted into too much detail about processes.

Consider the style of these paragraphs in the second part of the answer. They are very tightly written; informative, but

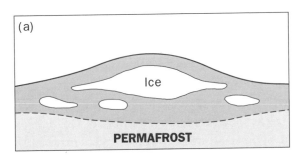
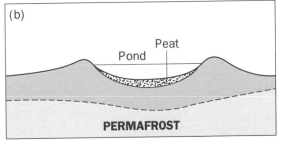

Figure 2 (a) Active pingo; (b) pingo rampart

with no irrelevant material — no 'waffle'.

Normally, you would be expected to give examples of any landforms described, but these are micro-features. Examples are therefore impossible to give. At the best, you could mention areas where such features occur.

As a general rule, new ideas and new information should not be introduced in the conclusion. In this

the thawing process. Due to its similarity to the sinkhole landscape of certain limestone regions, the term **thermokarst** is applied to this type of periglacial landscape. On a smaller scale, the presence of large numbers of small hummocks produced by frost heaving is another characteristic feature of periglacial regions. In Iceland, where such features are widespread, they are known as **thufurs**; elsewhere, simply as **tundra hummocks**.

A more spectacular effect of frost heaving is the creation of what is known as **patterned ground**. Repeated freeze–thaw cycles and the heaving of the ground have the effect of differentially sorting the soil materials. The simplest form of patterned ground, found on level or near-level surfaces, consists of **stone circles**. Fine material, such as sand and silt, tends to collect over small, slightly raised, freezing centres in the ground, and become surrounded by rings of stones and coarser material. Where several such rings join up with each other, a network of **stone polygons** may result. On sloping ground, this sorting process is also affected by the downslope movement of surface material, so that the polygons become progressively elongated, until, on slopes with a gradient in excess of 7°, they may eventually form **stone stripes**.

The downslope movement of surface material is particularly active in periglacial regions. The presence of permafrost effectively prevents the downward percolation of melt-water during summer, so that the active layer becomes highly waterlogged. The top of the permafrost acts as a lubricated surface over which the active layer tends to flow, even on the most gentle surfaces. This type of mass movement, known as **solifluction**, is one of the most characteristic and widespread processes operating in periglacial areas. It has the effect of filling hollows and valley floors with a deep layer of sludge, and produces lobate accumulations of soil and rock debris on hillsides. Its general effect is to give a smooth appearance to the landscape.

The smoothing effect of solifluction is in sharp contrast with the results of frost-shattering or **gelifraction**, which is another active process in periglacial environments. Exposures of solid rock are progressively shattered by the continual freezing and thawing of water in cracks and crevices, and may eventually be reduced to a series of sharp, angular pinnacles. In massively jointed rock, **tor-like** forms may be produced as a result of this same process. Weathered material will collect at the foot of cliffs to form accumulations of **scree**. Elsewhere, upland surfaces may become covered with angular, frost-shattered rock debris. Such areas are referred to as **blockfields** or **felsenmeer**.

It is clear that periglacial areas are distinguished by large numbers of distinctive landforms and minor surface features, most of them unique to that particular type of climatic environ-

ment. These features may be readily identified in active formation in high latitude regions and high mountain areas. However,
relict forms of these same features may also be found in areas
which no longer experience tundra-like conditions, but did so
during the Quaternary glaciation. 'Fossil' periglacial features,
such as the remains of ice wedges, pingos, stone polygons,
solifluction lobes, relict screes and blockfields, all provide important indicators of former periglacial conditions. The landscape
of contemporary Britain cannot be adequately explained without
reference to the legacy of periglacial activity in many areas.

case the rule is broken, and an
important point about relict
landforms is briefly mentioned. This
demonstration of an awareness of a
time dimension to the question
probably justifies a relaxation of the
normal conventions of examination
essay writing.

General comments

This question requires reference to a large number of technical terms. There is an extensive,
specialist vocabulary for describing landforms developed under periglacial conditions. Confusion
is sometimes caused by the fact that in some cases the same feature is designated by different
terms in different parts of the world. For example, surface mounds caused by internal ice
pressure are termed 'pingos' in Canada and 'pals' in Scandinavia. Make sure that you know
the technical vocabulary and use it with precision. Correct spelling is essential.

Related questions

1   To what extent is it possible to identify the effects of former periglacial processes in the
British Isles?

2   What is meant by the term solifluction? Describe the nature of the process and evaluate its
effects on landform development.

3   Describe the typical vegetation of Arctic and sub-Arctic environments, and show how it is
related to the conditions experienced in high latitude areas.

Question 5

How realistic is it to refer to a karst cycle of erosion?

Tackling the question

This question is concerned with the proposition that, subject to certain conditions, the landscape of karst (limestone) regions evolves through a sequence of identifiable stages. The implication is that the development of karst landscapes through time constitutes a special variation on the the so-called 'normal' sequence of landform evolution proposed a century ago by the pioneer geomorphologist, W.M. Davis.

The wording of the question suggests that what is required is a critical evaluation of this proposition. In order to do this effectively, you will need to consider not only the special processes operating in limestone areas, but also the general concept of the cycle of erosion. You will need to be familiar with the early views about landscape evolution, as well as the modern position which is critical of such a generalised model. Answers should include reference to the distinctive landforms of karst regions as well as type-areas. This is quite a demanding question.

Answer

A cautionary note is struck in the introduction. There are many different types of limestone with many different types of scenery and landforms.

In general terms, **limestone** may be defined as any rock consisting chiefly of carbonate of lime (calcium carbonate). One suggestion is that the term should be restricted to rocks containing more than 50% calcium carbonate. There are, in fact, innumerable types of limestone which may be distinguished according to mineralogical composition (e.g. dolomite or magnesian), texture (e.g. oolitic or pisolitic), origin (e.g. precipitated or corallian) or age (e.g. Carboniferous or Jurassic).

All limestones are particularly affected by chemical weathering but, because of their great variety, the resultant landforms are extremely varied. Thus, the Cretaceous chalk of Southern England is a relatively soft, pure, closely-jointed form of limestone which produces a very different type of scenery from that of the harder, denser, massively-jointed Carboniferous limestone of the Mendip Hills or Peak District.

Where limestone outcrops are thick, extensive and elevated, and where the water-table lies deep below the surface, particular types of landforms tend to develop. The term **karst** (or karst scenery) is used to describe this type of relief. The term karst is derived from the name of a barren limestone plateau located adjacent to the north-eastern coast of the Adriatic in former Yugoslavia. Landforms in this area were first described in the late nineteenth century by the Yugoslav geomorphologist, **J. Cvijic**, who naturally employed a number of Serbo–Croat words in his descriptions. Later, in 1921, Cvijic's work was translated and summarised by E.M. Sanders. It has been remarked that 'local British equivalents exist for most of the terms used to describe karst landforms, but these have never been systematically defined. As a result, writings on the subject are exasperatingly studded with Serbian and other words which have taken on the status of technical terms.' (S.W. Wooldridge and R.S. Morgan)

> This paragraph establishes when and where the concept of the karst cycle was first proposed.

The **karst cycle of erosion**, as described by Cvijic, makes three important assumptions: first, that there is a thick and extensive mass of pure limestone; secondly, that the limestone is covered by a surface layer of impermeable material which allows the initial development of a pattern of surface streams and rivers; and, thirdly, that the limestone mass is underlain by impervious rocks. According to Cvijic, during **youth** the impermeable surface layer is gradually removed by streams, and the surface drainage is progressively diverted underground down swallow-holes or 'dolines'. During the youthful stage, a system of underground drainage slowly develops, with extensive caves and connecting passages. Eventually, when there is no longer any surface drainage, maturity is reached. During **early maturity**, surface depressions in the limestone become progressively enlarged and may coalesce to form 'uvulas' and 'poljes'. In this way, the surface is gradually lowered. At this stage, the underground drainage displays three clearly-defined zones: an upper zone, in which water movement is always downward along vertical shafts or 'ponors'; a lower zone, in which drainage is predominantly horizontal and directed towards the margin of the limestone; and a middle zone, which, depending on the level of the water-table, is alternately one of vertical and horizontal movement of sub-surface water.

> The three conditions under which the karst cycle will develop, according to Cvijic, are identified prior to describing the four stages of the cycle. Characteristic landforms associated with each stage of the cycle are noted. Since many are relatively minor features, it is not possible to give specific examples.

Late maturity sees the underground streams reaching the impermeable rocks underlying the limestone. At the same time, the collapse of cavern roofs leads to a further lowering of the ground surface. Finally, according to Cvijic, in **old age**, surface drainage is re-established as the underlying strata are progressively re-exposed at the surface by the removal of the remaining limestone by weathering and erosion. During the old-age stage of the cycle, the limestone is reduced to a few residual masses or small hills known as 'hums'. Eventually, these too are removed to complete the cycle.

The karst cycle of erosion may be criticised on both general and specific grounds. That is to say, it is subject to all the same criticisms which may be levelled at the 'normal' or Davisian cycle of erosion, together with a number of specific criticisms which are particular to Cvijic's proposals for the idealised or theoretical landscape evolution of karst areas. It may be appropriate to consider the general criticisms first.

The concept of an ordered development of landforms, known as the **cycle of erosion**, or **geomorphic cycle**, was first proposed by the American geomorphologist W.M. Davis during the last decade of the nineteenth century. According to Davis, the development of landforms (as a result of weathering processes and fluvial erosion under humid conditions) may be divided into three stages — youth, maturity and old age. Youth is the stage of initial erosion on a new and rapidly-uplifted land surface. The landscape passes from youth to maturity when all traces of the initial surface disappear. Maturity is a stage of decreasing relief as the interfluves are gradually reduced in elevation. During old age, landforms become progressively more subdued and covered with a thick mantle of waste. A few residual hills (known as monadnocks) may rise up from this lowland which Davis termed a peneplain.

One point that may be made about the Davisian cycle, and the karst cycle too, concerns the enormous length of time during which base level must remain stable if the cycle is to run its course. Geological evidence suggests that the orderly progress of the cycle will be interrupted by events which will impose the development of a new cycle before the original has proceeded very far. The cycle may be upset in three main ways. First, large-scale changes of base level will initiate a new cycle, the relief forms of which will be superimposed on those of the original cycle. Secondly, climatic change, such as the onset of glacial or arid conditions, will cause a change in the processes of erosion operating on the landscape, which in turn will produce relief forms which are markedly different from those formed under the original conditions. Thirdly, large-scale vulcanicity will also interrupt the cycle by producing new constructional features which, because of the later date of origin, will not be in the same stage of the cycle as the landscape as a whole. In reality, most landscapes are polycyclic, the product of many partially complete cycles of erosion, and are far more complicated than those described by Davis.

Another criticism that may be levelled against both the 'normal' and karst cycles is that they are too concerned with generalisations about landform evolution, and largely ignore the processes operating in the landscape. 'The latter have often been

Having described the model, evaluation follows. The views expressed in the sample answer are generally critical. You could adopt a different position in your own answer, but would need to support it with appropriate arguments. What follows here are, firstly, criticisms of the concept of cycles of erosion in general, and then criticisms which are specific to the karst cycle.

taken as read, yet as soon as careful analysis of these processes is undertaken, their great complexity is realised, and what has often been regarded as axiomatic is revealed as untrue.' (R.J. Small) It has been suggested that acceptance of the cycle concept has led to studies of landscape evolution or denudational chronology being over-emphasised at the expense of process studies. Furthermore, uncritical acceptance of the cycle concept has hindered any serious attempt to prove that landforms actually do evolve towards the end form of the cycle, the peneplain. In practice, there are usually no grounds for the Davisian assumption that steep slopes are 'young' and gentle slopes are 'old'. It is also difficult to identify actual peneplain surfaces formed in the manner described by Davis. Several modern geomorphologists, such as J.I. Hack and R.J. Chorley, have suggested that so long as the factors which control denudational processes remain the same, landforms need not necessarily undergo any change. In other words, landform evolution is not an inevitable process. This type of argument stems from a new view of landform development known as 'dynamic equilibrium' which is at odds with many aspects of the older cycle concept. All of these general criticisms of the cycle concept apply equally to the 'normal' and karst cycles. In addition, a number of specific limitations of Cvijic's karst cycle may also be mentioned.

Reference to various writers in this paragraph (Small, Hack and Chorley) indicates background reading on the topic.

Unlike other cycles of erosion (the cycle of normal erosion, the cycle of periglacial erosion, the cycle of pediplanation, and the cycle of savanna erosion), the karst cycle describes the evolution of landforms on a certain rock type rather than under particular conditions of climate (humid, periglacial, arid or savanna). Furthermore, the large number of conditions laid down by Cvijic restrict the application and usefulness of his concepts. The limestone must be thick, elevated, relatively pure, underlain by impermeable strata, and also originally overlain by impermeable rocks. Many limestone outcrops fulfil none, or at best, just one or two of these conditions, thus rendering the karst cycle irrelevant for many limestone areas. Even in areas where the conditions are fulfilled, only some of the features described by Cvijic are found; others are absent. This is true of the Causses region of Southern France and the Peak District of Derbyshire. The karst cycle may help to explain the limestone features of Croatia and Slovenia, but appears to have limited application elsewhere. 'A cycle is, in effect, a model, or in other words an idealised representation of reality; and unless it has wide application it cannot be regarded as a very useful model.' (R.J. Small) Under these circumstances, it is probably not very realistic to refer to a karst cycle of erosion.

Rather late in the essay, reference is made to actual limestone districts which don't support the Cvijic model.

General comments

This is a very formal, traditional type of essay question. The title offers little or no help in deciding how the answer should be structured and organised. There is no 'task-word' (describe, evaluate, compare, examine, etc.) included in the title to provide guidance. Under these circumstances, special care should be given to essay planning. Spend a little extra time preparing the plan for the answer. Avoid a very fragmented answer with many short sections. Block your material together into solid, substantial paragraphs. As always, allocate one major theme per paragraph. Consider the sequence of paragraphs. Description should always come before evaluation and comment. Make sure that your essay has both an introduction and a conclusion.

Related questions

1   Write an explanatory account of the landforms associated with upland areas of Carboniferous limestone in the British Isles.

2   Why do the typical landforms of chalk and Carboniferous limestone areas differ?

3   Does the concept of 'cycles of erosion' have any real validity and usefulness in geomorphological studies?

uestion 6

> 'Although deserts are essentially low-rainfall areas,
> the role of water in shaping desert landforms should
> not be underestimated.' Discuss.

Tackling the question

The A-level geography examination inevitably includes questions on different types of physical environment. You will be expected to display a sound understanding of the process of landform development, not only in humid environments where fluvial processes are dominant, but also under various other conditions. These include landform development under glacial and periglacial conditions (see Question 4), as well as landform development in arid and semi-arid environments. This question is concerned with the latter.

Exam questions on deserts are mainly concerned with a discussion of the processes of landform development. You will almost certainly be expected to go beyond mere description of the distinctive landforms of arid regions, and should be prepared to evaluate the debates and different interpretations of their formation. Traditionally, the role of wind as an agent of erosion, transportation and deposition was considered to be all important. Currently, the role of water in shaping desert landforms is considered to be at least as important. You should be able to discuss the paradox that, although deserts are, by definition, low-rainfall areas, water action appears to have been important in producing many of their distinctive landforms. This particular question is typical of what to expect.

Answer

Guidance notes

Deserts are by definition low-rainfall areas. The conventional definition describes deserts as 'areas receiving less than 250 mm (10 inches) of rain per year'. However, such a definition based simply on total precipitation is not entirely satisfactory. It includes as 'desert' extensive areas of the Arctic and sub-Arctic which receive less than 250 mm of precipitation per year. Indeed, some texts refer to these high latitude areas as 'cold deserts'. A more satisfactory approach is to consider the relationships between precipitation received (P) and moisture lost by evaporation and transpiration by plants — evapotranspiration (Et). Since the amount of evapotranspiration varies with many

The problem of defining deserts is used as an introduction.

factors — in particular whether there is actually any water to evaporate — it is usual to estimate the amount of evapotranspiration which would occur from a standardised surface never short of water. This is termed potential evapotranspiration (PEt). In 1948, C.W. Thornthwaite devised an **index of aridity** based on the relationships between precipitation (P) and potential evapotranspiration (PEt).

When P = PEt throughout the year the index is 0.
When P = 0 throughout the year the index is –100.
When P greatly exceeds PEt throughout the year the index is +100.

Climates with an index of between –20 and –40 are described as semi-arid, those with an index below –40 as arid. Using these definitions, approximately 19% of the earth's land surface is classified as arid, and a further 14.6% as semi-arid. Areas of arid or desert climate include the Sahara Desert, the deserts of the Middle East and Central Asia, the Namib and Kalahari Deserts of Southern Africa, the Atacama and Patagonian Deserts of South America, the deserts of Mexico and South-West USA, and the Great Australian Desert. These are all areas of extremely **low, variable and unreliable rainfall**.

During the late nineteenth and early twentieth centuries, the landforms of such areas were explained largely in terms of wind action, with reference to features of wind erosion (deflation hollows, ventifacts, yardangs, zeugen, pedestal rocks, etc.) and deposition (dune formations of various types). Later, wind erosion came to be regarded as a relatively insignificant process, and increasingly desert landforms were seen as the product of very occasional but powerful rainstorms. However, in recent years, aerial and satellite photographs have revealed troughs and depressions consistently aligned with prevailing winds over extensive areas, and have led to a revival of many early ideas about the power of the wind as an agent of desert erosion and deposition. Currently, the relative importance of wind and water action in deserts is a subject of renewed debate and discussion.

The role of water in **desert weathering** has been the subject of many laboratory experiments and field observations. Even in deserts, some moisture is present from time to time, and may play a crucial role in weathering processes. For example, D.T. Griggs subjected a block of granite to alternate dry heating and cooling equivalent to 244 years of diurnal temperature change. At the end of the experiment, there was no detectable change in the rock. However, when cooled by a spray of water, the same rock started to crack after the equivalent of 2.5 years of diurnal temperature change. It was concluded that the presence of moisture may play an important part in the process

Using the Thornthwaite definition, a list of areas which form the subject of the essay is given in the penultimate sentence of this paragraph.

This paragraph identifies the two positions in the debate: wind action or water action?

Starting here, the arguments which support the role of water as being critical are set out in this and the following four paragraphs — one argument per paragraph.

of exfoliation. Studies of granite monuments in the Nile Valley show that statues near Cairo (where there is some slight rainfall) are more weathered than similar statues in drier parts of Egypt. It seems that chemical weathering in arid areas may be more important than had previously been assumed. In conditions of high evaporation various salts may accumulate near the surface. It has been suggested that the growth of salt crystals and their expansion when they take up water — a process known as hydration — may produce stresses in crystalline rocks and cause granular disintegration. Other rocks, notably clays and shales, experience slight changes of volume when wetted and dried. This, too, may cause such rocks to crack and split. Deserts frequently experience night temperatures well below freezing. For example, parts of the Mojave Desert in California have freezing temperatures on more than 100 nights per year. Thus, on those rare occasions when rain occurs, freeze–thaw action may operate even in deserts.

Despite their aridity, deserts are not totally devoid of **rivers**. Some are crossed by **allogenic** or **exogenous rivers** which have their source in humid areas, and, despite a progressive loss of discharge by evaporation and infiltration, maintain a course across the desert. Examples include the Nile and Colorado. Smaller rivers lose discharge until flow ceases or terminates in saline lakes. The River Jordan, for example, terminates in the Dead Sea. Thus, basins of **internal** or **endoreic drainage** are common in many desert areas. More typically, most rivers flow for only a short period after heavy rainfall. These are termed **ephemeral** or **intermittent rivers**. It is clear, therefore, that the role of fluvial processes cannot be totally discounted, even in regions where rivers are exceptional rather than normal.

Although deserts receive little rainfall, most rain that does occur is in the form of short-lived, torrential storms. For example, El Djem in Tunisia has a mean annual rainfall of 275 mm, yet storms there in 1969 produced 319 mm of rain in three days. In 1957, at Sharjah on the Persian Gulf, 70 mm of rain fell in just 50 minutes. Such torrential rain, falling on desiccated surfaces with a lack of protective vegetation, produces important landform changes. Short-lived surface flows of water can move vast amounts of sediment. Rainwash causes intense **sheet-** and **gully-erosion**. Desert valleys known as **wadis** in the Saharan region and **canyons** or **arroyos** in the American desert-lands, which remain dry for years on end, suddenly become occupied by rivers. The term **flash-flood** is given to this type of rapid run-off. Where rainwash is not concentrated in streams and rills, but spreads across a whole surface, the term **sheet-flow** is applied. It has been suggested that sheetflow may be instrumental in removing weathered material from the desert floor. Sediment transported by flash-floods is deposited where

Notice how each of these paragraphs includes reference to actual desert areas. You should aim for this combination of general, discursive material and supportive facts and examples.

The inclusion of detailed statistics and case material of this type will mark out the best quality answers. Obviously, solid revision is essential if you are to have any chance of doing this under exam conditions.

Notice the use of geographical vocabulary and technical terminology in this and the preceding two paragraphs.

The introduction of a temporal element will be a feature of the best answers.

In the light of the evidence presented, an attempt is made to draw some sort of conclusion in this final paragraph.

wadis and canyons open out onto adjacent lowlands. The result is a conical accumulation of coarse sediment known as an **alluvial fan**. Particularly good examples are found in the Basin and Range province of the Western United States; for example, along the margins of Death Valley in California. In places, large alluvial fans may coalesce to form a **bajada** or **alluvial apron** running continuously along the foot of the high ground. During rare desert rainstorms, the streams issuing from wadis and canyons may extend across and beyond the alluvial fan to reach a shallow saline lake known as a **playa**.

In many deserts, an extensive, gently-sloping erosional platform cut in solid rock lies between the mountain front and the playa basin. This feature is known as a **pediment**, and has been the subject of much controversy and debate, especially concerning its mode of origin. Reference to pediments is relevant in any discussion of the role of water in deserts, since at least two of the hypotheses put forward to explain pediment formation involve water action. Explanations include erosion by sheet-floods, erosion by meandering ephemeral streams, various weathering processes, and parallel retreat of the mountain edge. The weight of current opinion favours the latter process, which involves scarp retreat as a result of gully enlargement by occasional surface run-off. Eventually the upland is reduced to a few isolated, residual hills, known as **inselbergs**, which rise up from extensive pediments known as **pediplains**. Ayer's Rock in Australia is a well-known example. In North American deserts, these residual features are known as **mesas** and **buttes**. Spectacular examples are found in Monument Valley, Utah.

Finally, mention should be made of the action of water during earlier times in present arid areas. In addition to the short-term variations in precipitation described earlier, there is clear geological evidence to show that most desert areas have also experienced periods of increased rainfall in the past. These are referred to as **pluvial periods**. There is evidence, for example, that 5,000–10,000 years ago Lake Chad stood about 40 m higher than its present level. It seems likely, therefore, that during such pluvial periods, water action may have been much more important than at the present time. If that is the case, then certain desert landforms might be interpreted as 'fossil' features produced under different climatic conditions from those of today.

For both the landforms and processes described above, it is clear that water has played, and continues to play, an important role in landform development in arid lands. It appears to play a vital role in many processes of desert weathering. Furthermore, although deserts are relatively dry, they still carry drainage systems. It has been suggested that 'desert drainage basins, and the landforms within them, are not fundamentally different from those in more temperate climates. The differences which do exist are essentially ones of degree.' (R.U. Cooke) Various desert landforms, such as alluvial fans, which indisputably result from fluvial action, confirm that 'the role of water in shaping desert landforms should not be under-estimated'.

General Comments

The question requires you to discuss the role of water in the formation of desert landforms. At the planning stage you therefore need quickly to identify and jot down some of the opinions and debates on this topic. Early studies assumed wind action to be all important. Is that view still held? Are occasional rainstorms more important than the constant action of the wind? Could both processes be important? Is it necessary to reject either one? Was water action important in the past, even if insignificant now? Did desert landforms develop under different circumstances from those of today? Out of these first thoughts a plan should start to emerge. Having identified some of the discussion points, you then need to arrange them into a coherent essay structure.

Related questions

1 'Landforms show considerable variation from one desert region to another.' With reference to examples, suggest why this should be so.

2 Make a critical evaluation of the role of the wind in shaping desert landforms.

3 What is meant by the term 'desertification'? Examine the role of *either* human activity *or* climatic change in the process of desertification.

Question 7

What lessons can be learnt from the San Francisco earthquake of 1989?

Tackling the question

This is an unusual, but by no means unknown, type of question. It relates to a case study of a single, specific event: namely, the San Francisco earthquake of 1989. Such questions, when they appear, are generally concerned with a recent and still relatively-topical event. So, a question on the Soufrière eruption on Montserrat (1997) is certainly a better bet than one on Krakatoa (1883). Similarly, a question on the current flood-control and hydro-electric power developments on the Yangtze is more likely than one on the building of the Aswan Dam and hydrological works on the Nile. You must be alert to and mindful of current events and their potential for A-level examination questions. Obviously, there is a time lag before such case materials feature in textbooks, so you need to look elsewhere for reliable, up-to-date material. Newspapers can provide a rich source of information, and you should constantly augment your notes with cuttings of relevant case material.

Answer

This opening paragraph makes an important point about balancing risk with advantage.

Ever since the San Francisco earthquake of 1906, the inhabitants of that city have lived on a knife-edge, knowing that sooner or later the earth would one day move again, causing widespread devastation and destruction. San Francisco is built astride the San Andreas Fault which runs roughly north–south through this part of California, marking the boundary between the north-moving Pacific Plate and the south-moving North American Plate (Figure 1). In its broadest context, California forms part of the so-called 'Ring of Fire' which encircles the Pacific, and, as such, is constantly under threat from earth tremors, earthquakes and associated volcanic activity. On the other hand, the Bay Area with its magnificent natural harbour, superb scenery and agreeable climate, offers outstanding compensating advantages. For the 5 million people living in the Bay Area, the equation underlying their daily life involves a balancing of the earthquake hazard against the environmental and economic advantages which the area has to offer.

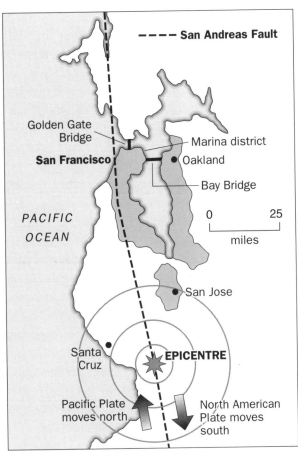

Figure 1 The San Francisco Bay Area in relation to the San Andreas Fault

It is not unreasonable to expect that you might include a similar map in such an answer. It serves to locate the position of the San Andreas Fault in relation to the Bay Area, together with the epicentre of the earthquake and the location of one or two places mentioned in the essay. Your map, drawn under examination conditions, will be less precise and less well drawn, but ought to convey the same amount of information.

On the occasion of the 1906 earthquake, there was a 7 m displacement along the line of the San Andreas Fault. The earthquake measured 8.3 on the Richter Scale, and more than 400 people died, mainly as a result of the collapse of large numbers of buildings across the city and the widespread fires which followed. Since then the city has been in a state of constant alert for a repetition of the 1906 catastrophe. From time to time minor rumblings and small earth tremors sent an ominous warning of what might be in store. The question to be considered, therefore, concerns the extent to which municipal authorities (civil engineers, architects, planners emergency services, etc.) can plan to minimise the destruction and loss of life caused by a major earthquake. Although inevitable, earthquakes are impossible to forecast in terms of precise timing, location or extent.

In 1906 almost all fatalities occurred within buildings. Clearly, therefore, the development of 'shock-proof' structures was a high priority for those engaged in the city's redevelopment programmes. Ever since 1906, the city authorities have been updating their 'safe building codes'. Techniques for high-rise buildings include extraordinarily deep foundations (as much as 25 m into bedrock), the insertion of joints into floor beams

This and the following paragraph identify ways in which preparations can be made to counteract the effects of natural hazards such as earthquakes.

This paragraph is essentially a description of the events of the earthquake.

The remainder of the essay focuses on the lessons to be learnt. Apart from problems caused by the design of elevated highways, the city fared relatively well. On the other hand, the closing sentences of the final paragraph sound a precautionary note. Probably the most important lesson to be learnt is not to be complacent.

which allow buildings to move, and the insertion of bearings and slider-plates between buildings and their foundations to provide 'seismic isolators'. In less spectacular ways too, the authorities have tried to prepare for the inevitable catastrophe. The San Francisco telephone directory has long contained a page of advice on what to do in an earthquake emergency. Local **emergency services** regularly carry out drills in response to simulated disasters (collapse of the Bay Bridge, fires, city-wide power failures, etc.), and many citizens take out earthquake **insurance policies**. In other words, San Francisco has long been in a state of alert, waiting for 'The Big One'.

Disaster struck at 5.04 p.m. on 18 October 1989. The epicentre of the earthquake was located near Santa Cruz, about 50 km south of San Francisco Bay. The tremors lasted for a mere 15 seconds and measured 6.9 on the Richter Scale. At least five aftershocks followed the main tremors. Cracks more than 3 m wide opened up on the streets; skyscrapers swayed by as much as 2 m; windows shattered in shops and offices; buildings toppled in Santa Cruz and San Jose near the epicentre, and some property collapsed in San Francisco itself. Gas mains fractured and caused fires in the Marina district; similarly, electricity cables and water mains were ruptured, and power and water supplies were cut off. The spectacular Golden Gate suspension bridge survived intact, but sections of the more mundane cantilevered Bay Bridge, which traverses shallow water, collapsed, as did extensive sections of the elevated Interstate Highway 880 (the Nimitz Highway) in Oakland. Altogether the cost of repairing structural damage in the Bay Area was estimated at $10 billion.

The most obvious lesson to be learnt from the 1989 earthquake is that 'shockproofing' of buildings really does work. Virtually all of San Francisco's modern buildings survived with only superficial damage. Hundreds of high-rise office blocks swayed, but finished upright and intact. The worst damage to property was in the Marina district where older buildings had been erected on sand reclaimed from San Francisco Bay. Clearly, areas of landfill provide unsuitable foundations for buildings in earthquake-prone regions, and should be put to other uses. It was also in the Marina district that fractured gas mains and resultant fires caused most damage.

By far the greatest loss of life occurred, not inside buildings, but in private cars travelling in the evening rush-hour on **elevated motorways and bridges** when the earthquake struck. The Nimitz Highway in Oakland, a double-deck structure built in the 1950s, suffered major collapse. More than 1,500 m of the upper deck fell onto the lower deck, crushing hundreds of cars and the occupants on the lower level. In the aftermath of the earthquake, accusations were made about faults in both the design and construction of the Nimitz Highway. A more obvious conclusion would seem to be that elevated highways and double-deck motorways are inappropriate structures in earthquake-prone regions. Unfortunately, Los Angeles, San Francisco and other Californian cities have long dedicated themselves to this type of urban road system. A close examination of existing elevated highways will be necessary, and a halt may need to be called to further building of this type.

In retrospect, the most striking fact about the San Francisco earthquake of 1989 was not how much, but how little damage it caused. When an earthquake of similar intensity hit Armenia in the previous year (1988), an estimated 25,000 died, and a whole town, Spitak, disappeared. In San Francisco, life returned to normal for most inhabitants within a matter of days. Gas, electricity and water supplies were quickly restored, and the city's underground rail system, criticised as an earthquake risk when it was built in the 1960s, suffered no damage whatsoever. The final **death toll** in an area of 5 million people was closer to 100 than the 400 originally estimated. Fewer than 20 of those deaths occurred away from the collapsed highway. As one commentator put it, 'This was a success story for Californian ingenuity, foresight and resilience. If the I-880 had stood up — as it should have done — this would have been an outright triumph of man over nature'. At the same time, the US Geological Survey announced that 'this was a far smaller earthquake than that of 1906. This was not The Big One. The Big One is still to come'. The lesson from that statement concerns the **unpredictability** of the Californian predicament and the need for constant **awareness** and a high state of **preparation** for dealing with further earthquake disasters.

General Comments

Virtually all the material contained in this essay was derived from contemporary newspaper reports of the 1989 San Francisco earthquake. There is plenty of good geographical information here. There are details of the tremors and aftershocks, references to different types of damage in different parts of the city, estimated costs of repairs and rebuilding, details of the death toll, etc. Districts are mentioned by name, and reference made to specific bridges and highways in the Bay Area. Comparisons are made with the 1906 earthquake. There is more than enough material here for a good answer, and it was all derived from newspaper reports.

Related questions

1 With reference to any one example, examine the causes and consequences of earthquake activity.

2 Discuss the view that 'the indirect results of volcanic eruptions frequently cause greater destruction and devastation than the volcanic activity itself'.

3 Many regions of crustal instability are among the most densely populated parts of the world. Explain why that should be the case.

Question 8

Examine the influence of ocean currents on the climate of adjacent coastal areas.

Tackling the question

Ocean currents, which may be warm or cold, influence the climate of adjacent coastal areas in a variety of ways. They have obvious effects on temperature, may cause or prevent the formation of sea ice in winter, determine amounts of precipitation, and may produce frequent and persistent sea mist and fog. In other words, you must include much more in your answer than just a consideration of effects on temperature. Many students answering this question never go beyond the obvious, and even fail to do that convincingly, with no more than passing reference to just one or two ocean currents and a couple of temperature statistics. You will need to produce more than just a couple of sides of vague waffle on the Gulf Stream.

The 'task-word' in the question is 'examine'. Think what that means. The word is not 'describe'. The question requires a detailed consideration of oceanic influences on climate. It requires an examination of the meteorological processes involved, reference to a range of ocean currents, and the inclusion of climate statistics for a number of shore stations.

Answer

Guidance notes

The atmosphere and the oceans are in a state of dynamic equilibrium. That is to say, the atmosphere and the oceans are closely inter-linked and inter-related. Ocean currents are both controlled by and contribute to global climatic conditions. On the one hand, the pattern of ocean currents is set in motion largely by the prevailing winds associated with the general circulation of the atmosphere. On the other hand, the currents themselves help to transfer heat from low to high latitudes, modify the extremes of climate, and play a vital role in maintaining the atmospheric heat balance.

Before examining the effects of ocean currents on climate, it may be useful to identify the main features of the circulation

The answer starts with a global overview of the inter-relationships between oceanic circulation and climate.

The scale of discussion changes in the second paragraph. The answer becomes more focused and detailed, looking at the causes and characteristics of warm and cold ocean currents.

of surface waters in the oceans. Ocean currents are caused by the frictional drag of air blowing over the surface of the water. The **general pattern** is therefore determined by the pressure and wind belts over the globe. The Coriolis Force produced by the earth's rotation deflects the direction of movement clockwise in the northern hemisphere. Obviously, the direction of movement is also affected by the configuration of the ocean basins. Temperature differences also affect the movement of water through their influence on density. Cold, relatively dense, water sinks toward the ocean floor and is replaced by an in-flow of warmer surface water from elsewhere. In very broad terms, it is possible to identify two major circular movements in the Atlantic and Pacific Oceans and to a lesser degree in the Indian Ocean. These are termed **gyres**. One lies north of the equator and one to the south. Between the two is an equatorial counter current.

The material contained in this diagram is very basic. You should be able to construct something similar in the examination. On the other hand, you may consider that a diagram is unnecessary. In that case you would need to elaborate on the final two sentences in paragraph two.

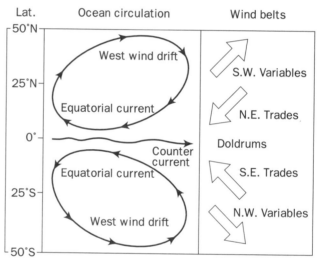

Figure 1 Schematic representation of wind-driven circulation showing two gyres

Where the west-flowing equatorial currents encounter the east coast of large land masses, they turn polewards and form warm currents running roughly parallel with the coasts. Examples include the Gulf Stream, the Brazilian Current and the Kuroshio Current. Coastal areas adjacent to these warm waters have higher than average temperatures. West wind drifts are deflected either polewards or equatorwards where they meet the west coast of large land masses. Thus, the North Atlantic Drift continues northwards beyond the British Isles to warm the coast of Norway, while the Canaries Current swings south along the coast of North-West Africa. In addition to these major circular flows and their extensions, there are a number of important cold currents in high latitudes in the northern hemisphere. These flow south from the Arctic Ocean through a series of straits leading to the Atlantic and Pacific Oceans. These cold currents

Lots of examples mentioned here: nine different ocean currents in a single paragraph. Good relevant detail.

include the Kamchatka Current which flows south from the Bering Strait, the Labrador Current which flows south from the Davis Strait, and the Greenland Current which flows south between Greenland and Iceland.

Coastal areas adjacent to warm or cold off-shore currents obviously experience a modification of their temperature conditions. What is less clear is the extent of that modification. Some examples will serve to give an indication of the scale of the influence exercised by ocean currents. In Southern Africa, the coastal towns of Mozambique and Benguela are both situated at roughly the same latitude, but are influenced by warm and cold currents respectively. Mozambique on the shore of the Indian Ocean is washed by the warm, south-flowing Mozambique Current, while Benguela on the Atlantic coast lies adjacent to the cold, north-flowing Benguela Current. Temperature statistics reveal a difference of about 6°C between the two towns at all seasons.

> This is a well-chosen example. It brings together the climatic influence of both warm and cold currents in a single region.

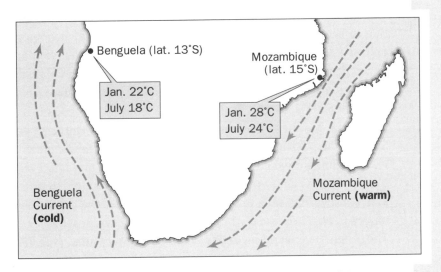

Figure 2 The influence of ocean currents on two coastal towns

Another way of considering the influence of ocean currents is by comparing station figures with an average for the same latitude. The difference between the two is known as a **temperature anomaly** and can be positive or negative. Thus, the Lofoten Islands, located north of the Arctic Circle at latitude 68°N but washed by the warm waters of the North Atlantic Drift, have the highest positive temperature anomaly in the world in January, 25.5°C warmer than the average for their latitude. The Lofoten Islands remain ice-free in winter, while the Newfoundland coast of Canada, chilled by the cold Labrador Current, is firmly ice-bound, despite being located a full 20 degrees of latitude further south.

The influence of ocean currents on the temperature regime of **inland locations** might next be considered. In fact, this varies

> This is a well-known and over-used example. On the other hand, it provides one of the most spectacular examples of temperature modification in the world.

> Although the question is about 'adjacent coastal areas', this

paragraph examines how far inland the moderating effect of the sea extends. The conclusion is that it depends on prevailing winds and coastal topography.

This is the material which is missing from many student answers. There are impacts, other than temperature, which must be examined with reference to appropriate locations.

widely from one area to another, and is determined by the direction of prevailing winds and the nature of the inland terrain. If the prevailing wind is offshore, the influence of an ocean current will be very limited and will not extend far inland. For example, the cold winter climate of New York City is essentially the product of interior conditions in North America and is hardly influenced by the warm waters of the Gulf Stream flowing offshore. On the other hand, prevailing onshore winds may carry oceanic influences far inland over interior districts. Mountain barriers will obviously restrict the influence of ocean currents to a narrow coastal strip. In Alaska, for example, the coastal town of Anchorage remains ice-free in winter, but Fairbanks on the interior lowlands, shut off from the sea by the Chugach and Alaska Ranges, has a bitterly cold mean January temperature of −25°C.

Ocean currents may also have an effect on the **cloud cover** and **precipitation** of adjacent coastal areas. This is particularly the case when cold ocean currents or upwellings of cold water are found offshore. In that situation, air moving onshore (either due to the prevailing wind or as a daily sea-breeze) becomes chilled as it crosses the cold water. If sufficiently chilled so that its temperature is reduced to dew-point, it will become saturated with water-vapour and cause fog or low cloud. **Sea mist** and **fog** is a characteristic feature of the cold water coasts of California, Southern Peru and South-West Africa. The case of San Francisco is well-known. In summer, thick sea mists, pulled in through the break in the coastal hills by the low pressure over the hot Central Valley to the east, pour through the Golden Gate and spill over the hills to the west of the city. As the chilled air moves inland it is warmed, and the mist and fog clear rapidly. The progressive warming of chilled air as it moves inland means that it becomes increasingly stable. The chance of rain being generated in that situation is negligible. Thus, many desert areas are associated with the presence of a cold ocean current or an upwelling of cold water offshore. Such is the case of the Atacama and Namibian Deserts.

From the preceding remarks, it will be clear that the influence of ocean currents on climate is very considerable. At a global scale, ocean currents play a vital role in maintaining the atmospheric heat balance, and therefore indirectly influence the climate of many regions. At regional and local scale, ocean currents can create distinctive regimes of temperature and precipitation. The extent to which those climatic regimes extend inland depends on a combination of local circumstances, including the direction of prevailing winds and the nature of the inland terrain.

General comments

Topics such as the influence of planetary wind systems on oceanic circulation, or the influence of ocean currents on the climate of adjacent shore areas, are very basic and straightforward. The processes involved are easy to understand and describe, and present few problems. On the other hand, high-scoring answers on these topics require a great amount of detailed information. There would be absolutely no point in attempting to answer the sample question unless you had at your disposal a selection of climate statistics to illustrate the effects of both warm and cold ocean currents. In other words, there is a strategic decision to be made. Either you make the effort to learn the relevant detail which you can then reproduce in the exam, or you decide to avoid this topic if it comes up in the exam.

Related questions

1   Write an explanatory account of the pattern of surface circulation in *either* the North and South Atlantic Ocean *or* the Pacific Ocean.

2   Examine the role of ocean currents in maintaining the global heat budget.

3   Make an evaluation of the direct and indirect effects of the North Atlantic Drift on the maritime nations of Western Europe.

Question 9

(a) Under what circumstances do temperature inversions occur?
(b) Describe the effects of inversions on weather conditions.

In essence these two questions seek facts and information. Part (a) requires you to identify the meteorological processes causing temperature inversions, and part (b) simply asks for a description of the weather conditions resulting from those processes. There is no requirement to evaluate or discuss; you must simply identify and describe.

With this sort of factual question it is relatively easy to score average marks, but difficult to really 'shine'. What, therefore, can be done to lift an average answer into a first-class answer? One way is to make sure that your answer plan is clear, logical and comprehensive. Make sure that all the relevant processes and all the relevant effects are included and presented in a logical sequence. Pay attention to clarity of expression. Complicated meteorological processes are not easy to describe, so try to make sure that your writing is accurate and precise. As always, the inclusion of some well-chosen examples and case material will help to lift your mark.

Answer

A definition of temperature inversions and some of their characteristics makes an adequate, if somewhat predictable, introduction to the answer.

(a) 'The temperature of the air normally gets lower with increasing height, but occasionally the reverse is the case. When temperature increases with height there is said to be an inversion.' (Meterological Glossary) Temperature inversions typically occur in narrow valleys or in enclosed hollows or above plains with adjacent hills and mountains. They tend to occur more frequently in winter than in summer and are particularly associated with winter anticyclonic calms.

In the answer to part (a) a distinction is made between low-level and high-level inversions. They are given one paragraph each.

There are two main causes of low-level temperature inversions: first, air at the lowest level of the atmosphere becoming chilled by contact with a cold surface; and, secondly, descending cold air becoming trapped in a hollow or narrow valley. These two mechanisms will be described in turn. During cold, dry, winter nights with clear skies, rapid heat loss by radiation takes place from the ground surface. As a result, the ground becomes intensely cold and, in turn, chills the lowest layers of the air above it. This effect is most pronounced in calm conditions, as any wind has the effect of mixing the air and equalising the temperatures of its lower layers. Temperature inversions of this type are common over snow-covered surfaces; consequently, low-level inversions occur frequently in polar regions. The depth of such inversions is rarely more than a few hundred metres, and often less. In many mountain and upland districts, dense cold air frequently moves downslope at night, becoming channelled along valleys to produce **katabatic winds** (anabatic winds move upslope during the day). The cold air associated with katabatic winds may accumulate in valley bottoms and hollows, especially if 'trapped' by topographical features or built structures lying across the valley floor. The result is the creation of a localised temperature inversion, with cold air lying beneath warmer air above.

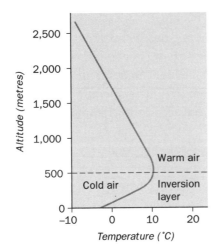

You could easily improvise and make up a similar hypothetical example in the examination.

Figure 1   A low-level inversion. In this case, the inversion extends to a height of about 500 m

High-level temperature inversions can also occur in the atmosphere. These usually result from the temperature changes which occur in subsiding air masses. Subsiding air gains heat by compression, and, as a result, may actually become warmer than the air beneath it. Large-scale, high-level inversions of this type are particularly associated with slow-moving anticyclonic pressure systems, such as those which form over continental land masses during winter months. The subsiding air within an anticyclonic system produces very stable conditions. **Subsidence** or **anticyclonic inversions** of this type show up very clearly on a **tephigram** (temperature–height diagram). They first appear at high levels and then slowly descend to within 500–2,500 m of the surface, where they may remain stationary for several days or more. Even if the lower air is turbulent, the inversion creates a blanketing effect by preventing convectional updraughts reaching any great height. High-level inversions can also result from other causes. For example, during the occlusion stage of a depression, warm air is pushed upwards by cold air which is undercutting it. At this stage, relatively warm air is found at height, and relatively cold air close to the surface. The **occlusion inversion** is, of course, a far less persistent feature than the anticyclonic inversion described above.

The description of the effects of inversions on weather conditions starts here. It involves reference to frost hollows, radiation fog and mist, urban smog and air stability.

This is a well-documented example. It appears in innumerable textbooks on meteorology.

(b) Temperature inversions influence weather conditions in a variety of ways. Areas affected by low-level inversions (produced by katabatic winds) experience night temperatures significantly lower than those of adjacent areas. Valley floors and enclosed hollows persistently affected in this way are referred to as **frost hollows**. An interesting example is that of the Chess Valley between Rickmansworth and Chorleywood in Hertfordshire. The valley is deeply incised into the surrounding hills and is blocked at its lower end by a high railway embankment. At night, a flow of cold katabatic air descends along the valley from the main Chiltern ridge and collects behind this embankment to produce exceptionally cold night temperatures. No month is immune from air frost, and night temperatures as low as –17°C have been recorded on occasions. Temperatures in this valley are among the most severe in the whole of Britain, rivalling those of mountain valleys in Scotland.

Another weather condition associated with low-level inversions is **fog**. This occurs when very moist air is cooled below its dew-point. The cooling does not involve uplift of the air, but takes place *in situ* by contact with a cold ground surface. Air close to ground level is trapped by the inversion so that there is very little horizontal or vertical movement. Fog caused in this way is termed **radiation fog**. It is particularly associated with cold, clear nights in autumn and winter. Its persistence depends on the thickness of the inversion layer, but usually it disperses quite quickly as incoming radiation from the sun warms up the ground, then breaks up the inversion. An increase in wind speed or turbulence will also have the same effect. When temperature inversions develop over urban areas, various pollutants — dust, smoke, exhaust emissions — become trapped beneath the inversion layer to create chemical fog or **smog** conditions. For example, 'On 5 December 1952, an anticyclone settled down over the London area. The whole Thames Valley was occupied by a pool of cold, stagnant air to a depth of 60–150 m, separated by a sharp boundary from warmer air above. Thus, London was sealed on either side by chalk hills, and above by an impenetrable inversion. A natural fog of water drops formed in this enclosed space, but to this was added the dirty smoke from London's innumerable chimneys which accumulated from day

This is a dramatic example of the effect of a temperature inversion on an urban micro-climate.

to day' (C.E.P. Brooks). The London smog of December 1952 lasted for four days, during which time visibility was no more than a few metres. An estimated 6,000 people died from bronchitis, pneumonia and other respiratory diseases directly attributable to the smog.

Finally, mention should be made of the effect of high-level inversions on **air stability**. The normal decrease of air temperature with height is known as the environmental lapse rate. The rate at which a rising air mass actually cools is known as the **adiabatic lapse rate**. This varies according to whether the air is dry or saturated. If, at any given height, rising air is warmer (and therefore lighter) than the surrounding air, it will continue to rise; that is to say, it is unstable. However, at a temperature inversion, any rising air will be surrounded by considerably warmer air and will sink back again. In other words, high-level inversions create very stable conditions, impose an upper limit on updraughts of air, and reduce the possibilities of precipitation. Inversion levels which determine the limits of upward air movements also influence the height and thickness of cloud layers, the upper cloud level corresponding with the inversion.

In summary, temperature inversions may occur either at very low or high levels in the atmosphere. The former are the result of radiation cooling of the ground or katabatic air flow, whereas the latter are most usually due to subsiding air masses. Low-level inversions create **local weather effects** — frost, mist, fog and smog — while high-level inversions have **regional effects** on weather, in particular by imposing stable conditions over wide areas.

The conclusion is a very tightly written summary of some of the main points raised in the main body of the essay.

General Comments

This is rather like the previous question — conceptually easy, but impossible to answer well without a great deal of detailed factual information. You need to be able to make reference to actual locations, provide examples and case studies and be able to illustrate points of explanation with actual temperature statistics. So, again, a strategic decision is required. Either make a big revision effort or avoid the topic. You should also be prepared for a question on temperature inversions in the data-response section of your exam. A question on the interpretation of an actual tephigram would be the sort of thing to anticipate.

Question 9

Related questions

1 Episodes of severe urban atmospheric pollution are almost always associated with temperature inversions. With reference to examples, elaborate on this assertion.

2 Compare and contrast the effects of high-level and low-level temperature inversions on weather conditions.

3 Examine the various meteorological conditions which produce fog and mist.

Question 10

Examine the effects of large cities on local climates.

Tackling the question

The whole field of microclimatology is a popular one with A-level examiners. Of the various topics available for testing in this subject area, none is more popular than that of urban microclimates. If your syllabus includes work on meteorology and climatology, this is a good topic to revise. The effects of large cities on local climates are quite straightforward and easy to describe and explain. You need to mention the creation of 'heat islands', thermal uplift and urban thunderstorms, atmospheric pollution and changes in the composition of the atmosphere above and downwind of large cities. This last theme includes reference to the old-fashioned type of urban smog, as well as the more recent phenomenon of photochemical smog. Organise your answer so that each of these themes constitutes a good solid paragraph.

However, the key to a good answer is the inclusion of plenty of examples. You need to refer to actual towns and cities, and to actual climate statistics. So, make sure that your revision for this topic involves memorising case material. This sample answer makes detailed reference to the urban climates of London and La Porte, Indiana, as well as passing reference to New York, Los Angeles and Mexico City. You should have no problem finding information about the local climate of these and other towns and cities. Read the sample answer carefully, and notice how general descriptive and explanatory material is combined with specific references to actual towns and cities. You should aim for that same mixture and balance in your own essays.

Answer

Superimposed on the general climate of any region are small-scale local variations produced by differences in aspect, type of ground surface cover, the presence of lakes and other large water bodies, and so on. The study of these local variations is known as **microclimatology**. In recent years, much research in micro-climatology has been concerned with the distinctive local climate of large cities. Large cities generate dust, radiate heat, have only a limited vegetation cover, and contain high buildings which modify the frictional characteristics of the ground surface. These, and other human-made modifications to the

Guidance notes

The introduction defines the subject area, and in very general terms suggests why urban climates differ from those of adjacent rural areas. These general points are then picked up in turn in the main body of the essay which follows.

The 'heat island' effect is considered to be the most important and best documented of the special features of urban climates, and is given three paragraphs in the plan. Other characteristics are allocated one paragraph each.

natural environment, combine to produce urban climates which are significantly different from those of adjacent rural areas.

First, the effect of large cities on **temperature** conditions may be considered. Built-up areas absorb more solar radiation than adjacent rural areas. Dark coloured roofs, the brickwork and stonework of buildings, and the tarmac of city streets have a large thermal capacity and good conductivity. Heat tends to be absorbed and stored during the day and released at night. In addition, cities also produce a good deal of artificial heat from industrial processes, as well as commercial and domestic central heating systems. Because of their generally higher temperatures, large cities are often referred to as '**urban heat islands**'. The temperature difference between town and country is usually greatest at night when buildings and roads release heat to the air around them. At dawn, urban temperatures are still higher than those of surrounding areas, but the countryside then warms more quickly than the city where buildings shade the ground from the early heat of the day. Within the city, temperature variations can be related to building densities, population densities, as well as the location of industry, parks, open spaces, reservoirs, etc. The rural–urban temperature differential is usually greatest under calm anticyclonic conditions. Strong winds have a tendency to disperse and reduce the effect of the urban heat island.

Although this is quite an old piece of research, the results are still relevant, and it is the most detailed work to have been carried out on London's climate.

During the early 1960s, **T.J. Chandler** carried out detailed research on the microclimate of London, the results of which were contained in his book *The Climate of London* published in 1965. According to Chandler, the centre of London has a mean annual temperature of 10.9°C compared with 10.2°C for the suburbs (Kew) and 9.7°C for the surrounding countryside. Maximum temperatures were shown to vary little between town and country, but minimum temperatures were found to be significantly different.

You may not be able to remember as much factual detail as this, but some temperature statistics are essential for the answer. You must establish the scale of the differences between city centre, suburbs and countryside.

	Max.(°C)	Min.(°C)	Mean (°C)
Central London	14.6	7.3	10.9
Suburbs	14.3	6.2	10.2
Surrounding countryside	14.0	5.5	9.7

The effects of the 'urban heat island' phenomenon are quite obvious. Frosts may be less frequent in the inner city than the suburbs; sleet may occur rather than snow in winter; any snow will lie for a shorter period than in the nearby countryside; more air conditioning may be needed in summer; indeed, summer heat, especially if combined with high humidity, may become highly oppressive for inner-city dwellers, leading in turn to an increase in aggressive behaviour and crime during prolonged summer heatwaves.

The effects of large cities on the amount, frequency and intensity of **precipitation** are more difficult to evaluate. Large built-up areas usually have **lower humidity** than nearby areas of open land. This reflects the general absence of vegetation and large bodies of open water, together with the rapid removal of surface water through drains and culverts, all of which cause reduced **evapotranspiration** over urban areas. On the other hand, it has been shown that the existence of an urban heat island can cause upward movements of air, a process which is encouraged by the presence of high-rise buildings. It has been suggested that **thermal uplift** and **turbulence** of this type can initiate **rain and thunderstorms**. The presence of particular pollutants in the atmosphere from industry may also provide the hygroscopic nuclei necessary in the rain-forming process. Analysis of long-term thunderstorm patterns for South-East England reveals a far higher frequency of thunderstorms over London than elsewhere. Another well-known example of the effect of urbanisation and industrialisation on local climate is that of La Porte in Indiana. La Porte is located 50 km downwind of the vast iron and steel-making complex around the south shore of Lake Michigan between Chicago and Gary. The town has experienced a 30–40% increase in the amount of precipitation, and similar increases in the frequency of thunderstorms and occurrence of hail since the 1920s when much of the present industrial plant was established.

This example is well documented and is described in many textbooks.

The **content of the atmosphere** above large cities also differs from that of most rural areas. Industrial and domestic chimneys and car exhausts emit enormous amounts of gaseous and solid impurities which pollute the atmosphere in and above large cities. The pollutants include soot, ash, sulphur dioxide (SO_2), carbon monoxide (CO), oxides of nitrogen (NO, NO_2, and NO_3) and other gases together with fumes and smoke. Much of this pollution drifts downwind from the city and also affects the climate of areas in that direction. The accumulation of atmospheric pollutants above large cities has a number of climatic effects. For example, there is evidence from Britain that skies over built-up areas tend to experience **thicker and more frequent cloud** than those of surrounding rural areas. This may be due to the increased turbulence over cities together with the increased condensation caused by pollution nuclei. Increased cloud in turn means **reduced amounts of sunshine**, another feature of urban climates. At ground level, tall buildings also cast their shade over considerable areas. This is particularly evident in cities such as New York with narrow, canyon-like streets flanked by skyscrapers.

Both forms of urban fog are described in this paragraph, the old type of smog caused by smoke emissions and the current type of photochemical smog caused by car exhaust emissions.

The incidence and density of **fog** are also clearly related to atmospheric pollution. Occasionally, under stable conditions, radiation fog may combine with high levels of pollutants in the atmosphere and become trapped under a temperature inversion layer to form thick, sulphurous, yellow fog known as smog. A well-documented instance of this process was the London smog of December 1952 which resulted in some 6,000 deaths from respiratory conditions in a single week. The worst of these smogs have now been eliminated, thanks to the establishment of 'smokeless zones' prescribed by the Clean Air Act of 1956. However, similar problems continue elsewhere. At La Porte, described earlier, the town suffers from an average 110 days per year with **smoke-haze**. There is also another type of urban fog known as **photochemical smog**. This involves chemical reactions in pollutants induced by sunlight. It is most common where there is large-scale combustion of petroleum products. Certain exhaust emissions are converted by sunlight into harmful substances such as ozone. Photochemical smog of this type is a well-known feature of the climate of Los Angeles and Mexico City. Both are dominated for long spells by sub-tropical anticyclones, sunny conditions and subsidence inversions. Both are bounded by hills, and both have a high density of cars and other vehicles. Photochemical smog is unpleasant, damages and destroys vegetation, causes irritation to eyes, and has been identified as a serious health hazard.

The effects of large cities on local climates are both numerous and well documented. Compared with rural areas, large cities experience higher temperatures, greater amounts of precipitation, more frequent thunderstorms, more cloud, less sunshine, and more frequent occurrence of fogs of various types. The scale of difference may be only small — one or two degrees of temperature or a few millimetres of rain — but the effects on the well-being and comfort of urban dwellers may be significant.

General Comments

From your point of view this is a high priority topic; one that is worth making a big effort to revise, simply because of the frequency of its occurrence. It falls within the general subject category of 'human impacts on the natural environment' which is highly favoured by examiners at the moment. The key to success is case material. Chandler's research on London's microclimate is a classic (if somewhat dated) study, but there is excellent material available on the notoriously polluted urban climates of Mexico City and Los Angeles. Careful revision of this topic could really pay off.

Related questions

1 In what ways, and why, do the climates of large urban areas differ from those of adjacent rural areas?

2 Write an explanatory account of the local climate of any one large city.

3 What are the main problems involved in improving air quality in large cities?

Question 11

Categories of air pollution

Category	Vertical scale	Temporal scale	Scale of organisation required for resolution
Local	Height of stacks	Hours	Municipal
Urban	Lowest mile	Days	County or multicounty
Regional	Troposphere	Months	State, provincial or national
Continental	Stratosphere	Years	National or international
Global	Atmosphere	Decades	International

(Source: Stern, A.C. et al. *Fundamentals of Air Pollution*. Academic Press. 2nd Ed. 1984)

(a) Write five short paragraphs giving examples of the type of atmospheric pollution typical of each of the categories or scales identified in the table. (15 marks)

(b) Select any *one* of the five categories and suggest what strategies might be necessary to control atmospheric pollution at that particular scale. (10 marks)

Tackling the question

This is an unusual question format. You are presented with a table showing the characteristics of five different categories of air pollution. The categories are based on different spatial scales, from local to global. For each category, you are provided with information about the vertical extent of the polluted layer, the typical duration of its occurrence, and the level of the authority required for its resolution.

Part (a) of the question asks for a single paragraph on each of the five categories in which you must provide 'examples of the type of atmospheric pollution typical of each of the categories'. This is a very straightforward, descriptive task. No explanation, or evaluation, or critical analysis; just simple description. Part (b) asks you to focus on any one of the five categories and discuss strategies for pollution control. Lots of choice there, and again, a question that should present few problems. The lesson is this: don't reject unorthodox questions out of hand. Don't be put off by unusual question formats. At first sight this question appears quite daunting. Closer examination shows that it is easier than most.

Answer

Guidance notes

(a) Examples of atmospheric pollution at different scales.

1. Local

At this smallest scale, the sources and receptors of pollution are in close proximity, typically in sight of each other. An example would be a line of vehicles emitting exhaust fumes along a busy urban street and polluting the lowest level of the atmosphere just above street level to the detriment of pedestrians and the occupants of the adjacent buildings (**receptors**). In this case the **sources** would be the traffic; the **pollutants** would be the exhaust fumes; the **diffusion mechanisms** would be air movements caused by the passage of the vehicles and local weather conditions; the **height** of the pollution would be largely determined by the pattern of local buildings; the **duration** might typically be measured in hours, reflecting the speed with which traffic volumes can change. In other instances the source of local pollution might be a single chimney stack emitting smoke or fumes over the immediate locality.

2. Urban

If levels of atmospheric pollution are monitored over urban areas for a long period of time, it will be found that on average, taking into account winds from different directions, pollution levels are highest over the inner city and decline outwards towards the suburbs and rural areas beyond. Large cities are normally ventilated by two processes: horizontal air flow which moves pollution laterally; and vertical convection currents which lift pollution to the upper levels of the atmosphere. However, on occasions both mechanisms fail simultaneously. For example, calm anticyclonic conditions may reduce lateral dispersion, while at the same time a temperature inversion may limit vertical air flow. The resultant build up of pollutants from domestic and industrial sources and vehicle exhaust emissions is referred to as a **pollution episode**. Los Angeles and Mexico City are notorious for pollution episodes of this type. Pollution above cities may extend vertically for more than an kilometre, and severe episodes may persist for several days.

3. Regional

Outside of urban and metropolitan areas the level of pollutants in the air is referred to as the **background concentration**. Normally this is significantly lower than that of urban areas. However, in Europe and North America there is clear evidence that the atmosphere of non-urban areas is becoming increasingly contaminated by the long-distance transmission of pollu-

Given the form of the question, there is clearly no requirement to write a formal essay answer. In the circumstances it is quite appropriate to present your answer with numbered sections and headings.

These are both well-known and over-used examples. Nevertheless, they are absolutely relevant.

Specific examples of air pollution at regional scale are difficult to identify. This paragraph is wholly generalised. Maybe you have an appropriate example, and could be more specific than this.

A-Level Geography: Essays

53

Question 11

tants from tall stacks. In addition, many rural activities, such as the burning of fields and agricultural waste and crop spraying, serve to increase the level of the background concentration. In many regions the non-urban air which used to 'flush' the major cities is itself already contaminated from other urban and rural sources of pollution. At this scale pollutants may extend throughout the whole vertical extent of the troposphere, and concentrations of pollutants may persist for months, rather than days or weeks, according to weather conditions.

4. Continental

During the last two decades or so there has been growing concern about the transportation of pollution across international boundaries. For example, much has been written about the movement of sulphur and nitrogen oxides from Britain to the Low Countries, Germany and Scandinavia where it is washed out of the air as **acid rain** which pollutes freshwater bodies and damages and destroys vegetation in the receptor countries. At a similar scale, pollutants from industrial centres in the US Mid-West and around the Great Lakes are carried north-eastwards to produce acid rain over Eastern Canada. Pollution at this scale is caused by emissions from any sources and extensive air masses are contaminated. Coal-burning power stations in particular are a major source of this type of pollution. Since the mid-1970s there has been a succession of joint-international studies and reports on the problem. There also exists a **Convention on Long-range Transboundary Air Pollution (1983)** signed by more than 20 nations, but no real progress has been made in dealing with the problem. At continental scale, pollutants may be carried into the stratosphere and may persist for a period measured in years.

5. Global

Currently much attention is focused on problems of atmospheric pollution at global scale. It is well known that the system of atmospheric circulation is able to transport particulate matter from volcanic eruptions or radioactive debris from nuclear explosions high into the stratosphere, and that much later such contaminants may return as 'fall-out' far from the original source. The current fear is that the build-up of pollutants is causing changes in the composition of the atmosphere which in turn are affecting global climates. A build-up of suspended particulate matter might reduce the amount of solar energy which reaches the earth's surface, thereby causing **global cooling**. Conversely a build-up of carbon dioxide which absorbs infrared radiation could reduce the amount of heat which

Acid rain is a serious contemporary problem. Be sure to learn and revise this topic. Here is a good opportunity to introduce it into the answer.

escapes into space as infrared radiation, thereby causing global warming (the so-called '**greenhouse effect**'). Both carbon dioxide and particulate matter have been increasing throughout the twentieth century, during which time the temperature of the earth has decreased very slightly. Possibly the opposing effects of the two pollutants have largely cancelled out each other, but clearly the balance is a very delicate one. Another matter of concern is the **depletion of the ozone layer** of the lower stratosphere by the release of fluorocarbons and nitrogen oxides (from exhaust fumes) into the atmosphere. The ozone layer is crucial in absorbing solar energy in the ultraviolet (UV) wavelengths. Increases in UV radiation will have serious effects on humans as well as flora and fauna.

Global warming and the so-called 'greenhouse effect' is another important current issue. This can be worked into the answer when writing about atmospheric pollution at global scale.

(b) Atmospheric pollution control at urban scale

A chronological survey of atmospheric pollution since the beginning of the Industrial Revolution forms a depressing catalogue of inaction and complacency in the face of relentless pollution damage to the earth's atmosphere. Long-term damage has constantly been excused or justified by the short-term profits of polluters or the costs of anti-pollution measures. It may be appropriate, therefore, to concentrate on one of the few success stories: namely the improvement of air quality in British cities during the postwar period.

During the nineteenth and early twentieth century, urban air pollution was largely a product of the burning of coal in industrial boilers and furnaces, steam locomotives and domestic fireplaces. There were other forms of pollution too, derived mainly from particular industries such as metal smelting and chemical production. As cities grew and industry expanded, the problems increased. The most obvious manifestation of the problem was the regular occurrence of devastating 'smogs' over many cities.

In December 1952 a major air pollution disaster brought London to a standstill for several days and was responsible for several thousand deaths. At last this provided the stimulus for action. As a result the powers of the Alkali Inspectorate (responsible for controlling industrial emissions) were greatly increased. More importantly, the **Clean Air Act (1956)** was passed. This required the establishment of **smokeless zones** in major cities, in which smokeless fuel had to be substituted for soft coal for domestic heating.

Increasingly too, from the early 1960s, central heating replaced open fires in British homes. By 1970 the concentration of both sulphur dioxide and particulate matter in the air above London had been reduced to less than one-third of the 1960

This is a brief review of the legislation which has been enacted to reduce urban smog in the UK. It also highlights the emergence of a new problem and the need for action to reduce petrochemical pollution.

level, and smogs had become a thing of the past. Similar transformations took place in cities such as Sheffield and Leicester which had previously suffered from chronic pollution. In 1966 an International Clean Air Congress was held in London, and soon after a national air pollution research centre was established at the Warren Springs Laboratory, Stevenage.

However, while there has been a reduction of pollution resulting from coal-burning (smoke, ash, dust, sulphur dioxide) there has been a simultaneous increase in pollution derived from vehicle exhaust emissions (carbon monoxide, unburned hydrocarbons, nitrogen oxides, lead, etc.). In a sense, therefore, one problem has been substituted for another. Control of industrial and domestic emissions has been relatively successful. The next stage forward will require legislation to control the content of vehicle fuels and the compulsory fitting of catalytic converters and other devices on vehicles to reduce the harmful effects of vehicle emissions.

General comments

The subject matter of this question is predictable, but the question format is unusual. Again, the question is concerned with human impacts on the natural environment; specifically, the pollution of the atmosphere at different spatial scales. Pollution at single city scale was mentioned in connection with the previous question. Here is another opportunity to use the same case material about the pollution problems of your selected city. Part 4 of the answer discusses acid rain, and part 5 is concerned with global warming. These are both absolutely essential topics for revision.

Related questions

1   'Pollution does not respect international boundaries.' Using examples, elaborate on this statement with reference to atmospheric pollution.

2   Write an essay on the causes and consequences of global warming.

3   Examine the processes involved in the creation of acid rain, and describe the effects of acid rain on both terrestrial and aquatic environments.

Question 12

The Caribbean region and the South-Eastern USA are regularly subjected to the impact of tropical hurricanes.

(a) Briefly outline the characteristics of such hurricanes. (5 marks)

(b) Identify the various types of damage caused by the passage of these hurricanes. (10 marks)

(c) Suggest ways in which the destructive effects of hurricanes might be minimised. (10 marks)

Tackling the question

With this type of question, the answer-planning is largely done for you. You don't have to identify key themes and arrange them in the best order, or even think about an appropriate introduction and conclusion as in a formal essay answer. In this case the themes are identified for you: the characteristics of hurricanes, the types of damage they cause, and the ways in which that damage can be minimised. The latter two themes each carry twice as many marks as the first one, and obviously require more attention and detail.

During the planning-time for the answer you should focus on content, making sure that you cover as many points as possible. Make lists. How many different types of hurricane damage can you think of? Have you missed any out? Since the examiners won't be awarding marks for structure, it is safe to assume that they will be giving extra credit for content, information and examples. Make sure that your answer is as comprehensive as possible.

Answer

Guidance notes

(a) Characteristics of hurricanes

The term hurricane refers to intense, tropical low-pressure systems which occur in the region of the Caribbean and South-Eastern USA. Identical features are known elsewhere as cyclones (Indian Ocean), typhoons (South China Sea) and willy-willies (Northern Australia). On weather charts they appear as exceptionally deep centres of low pressure (typically about 950 mb

After a few sentences dealing with definition and terminology, the answer starts to focus on the question, and begins to itemise the characteristics of tropical hurricanes. The catalogue of characteristic features is kept quite short, mainly because a diagram is included as part of the answer. You might feel that, since part (a) only carries five marks, a diagram is not justified.

but sometimes even lower) surrounded by tightly packed concentric isobars. Hurricanes vary in extent from 80 to 800 km across. Figure 1 shows typical features. At the centre is the **eye** of the hurricane (10–50 km across), an area of clear, dry, descending air. Around the eye is a 'cylinder' of rising air, dense cloud and heavy rain, at the base of which violent, rotating winds are being sucked in towards the eye of the hurricane. These devastating winds may reach speeds of well over 150 km/hour, with gusts of over 300 km/hour. The definition of a hurricane force wind, Force 12 on the Beaufort Scale, is one exceeding 115 km/hour.

Hurricanes normally develop in late summer and autumn over the warm tropical waters of the Mid-Atlantic, just north of the equator. Usually, they track westwards across the West Indies, swing northwards along the east coast of the USA, before turning west to die out over the cooler Atlantic waters of mid-latitudes. Hurricanes moving inland become cut off from the heat energy of the warm ocean waters, and usually die out rapidly. Thus, hurricanes represent a particularly dangerous hazard for the Caribbean islands and the low-lying coastal areas of South-East USA. On average, 11 hurricanes sweep across the region each year.

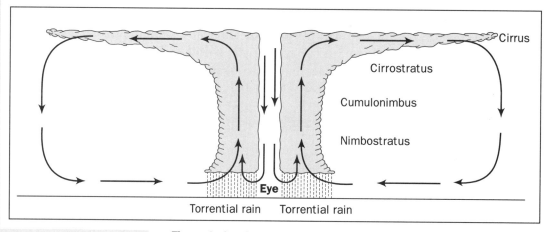

Figure 1 Section through a hurricane showing characteristic features

(b) Types of damage caused by hurricanes

The damage caused by the passage of a hurricane can be enormous. For example, Hurricane 'Diane' which swept across the Caribbean and Deep South of the USA in 1955 is estimated to have caused $1,000 million-worth of damage. With the migration of population to Florida and other 'sunbelt' states of the USA, the potential for property damage and loss of life by hurricanes increases year by year. Damage is not equally inflicted. In the West Indies many domestic and other buildings are poorly constructed (compared with the USA), and coastal defences are also of an inferior quality or non-existent. Thus, at individual and family level the hardship caused by hurricanes is often much greater among the West Indian population than among the American population which is better protected and 'insulated' from financial loss by insurance. Hurricane damage is essentially of three types: damage caused by **violent winds**, damage caused by **storm-surges**, and damage caused by **torrential rain**. These will be considered in turn.

1. Damage caused by violent winds
Hurricane-force winds obviously cause extensive **structural damage** to buildings in their path. Poorly constructed buildings may be completely demolished, or may have roofs lifted and blown off. According to one American insurance company, about 10% of all buildings lying in the central path of a typical hurricane will be destroyed beyond repair. Almost all buildings will suffer lesser damage such as broken windows, collapsed chimney-stacks and roof damage. Strong winds will also overturn cars, caravans and mobile homes, will fell telegraph poles, derail trains, uproot trees and destroy crops. In 1980, Hurricane 'Allen' destroyed 97% of St Lucia's banana plantations and 95% of St Vincent's.

Since this is not a formal essay answer, numbered lists of points with headings and sub-headings are acceptable. This style of presentation should be used sparingly in essays.

Notice how examples are worked into the answer. Three (Diane, Allen and Alice) are mentioned in part (b) of the answer.

2. Damage caused by storm-surges
Due to the changes in pressure, the passage of a hurricane will also cause a rapid rise in sea level, so that massive **storm waves** to heights of 10 m or more above the normal mean tide level may be driven onshore by the winds, sending floodwater far inland along low-lying coasts. Such storm-surges frequently cause more damage and loss of life than the winds themselves. Storm-surges demolish coastal properties, sink boats at anchor, carry away livestock, and cause deaths by drowning. In 1935 over 400 people died, almost all by drowning, during the passage of a hurricane across Florida.

3. Damage caused by torrential rain
Around the eye of a hurricane, rapidly rising air masses produce enormous vertical banks of cumulonimbus cloud and torrential rain, usually accompanied by thunder and lightning. For example, in 1954 Hurricane 'Alice' dumped an incredible 675 mm (27 inches) of rain over South-West Texas in just two days. Although this deluge was exceptional, the rainstorms associated with most hurricanes frequently cause rivers to overtop their banks and result in the widespread inundation of surrounding low-lying areas.

(c) Minimisation of hurricane damage

Reference to published work is a feature of the best answers. It is unlikely that you will be able to recall direct quotations as here, but it is often possible to encapsulate and summarise the ideas of key contributors to particular debates. The aim is to demonstrate that you have done some background reading on the subject.

It has been noted that 'faced with the need to exploit an inherently hazardous environment, and motivated by the challenge of doing so, man has developed various means of coping with hazards.... Adjustment to hazard threats is thus a basic feature of human survival and prosperity.' (C. Park) It has also been suggested by I. Burton, R.W. Kates and G.F. White (*The Environment As Hazard* 1978) that the theoretical response options to natural hazards are of three types:

1. Modify the cause or nature of the hazard;
2. Modify vulnerability to the hazard;
3. Redistribute the losses caused by the hazard.

The three types of damage reduction identified are considered in turn.

In the case of geophysical hazards and climatic hazards, such as hurricanes, the possibility of modifying or reducing the enormous natural forces involved is very limited indeed. Nevertheless, attempts have been made to reduce the severity of hurricanes. An early US experiment (Operation Stormfury) which began in 1960 involved flying planes into the eye of hurricanes in order to 'seed' the clouds with crystals of silver iodide. In this way it was hoped to speed precipitation over ocean areas and to reduce wind speeds. Results have been inconclusive, although the experimenters claim to have achieved a 10–15% reduction in the wind speeds.

A more realistic strategy to minimise hurricane damage involves modifying or reducing vulnerability to the hazard. This involves **strengthening the defences** against hurricane damage. This might be achieved in various ways; for example, by replacing flimsy wooden shacks with brick or stone-built dwellings, adding shutters to all windows, producing well-made, solidly-constructed buildings, raising and strengthening sea-walls and river banks and levees, and siting all new buildings well back from the beach front where the worst damage is likely to be caused by storm-surges. In Miami Beach, which receives on average one hurricane every seven years, all new buildings are raised on artificial mounds 6 m above mean sea-level as a minimum protection against storm-surges.

This response to the hurricane hazard in Miami provides an appropriate example for this section of the answer.

Early warning and tracking of approaching hurricanes is now an essential part of the strategy to reduce vulnerability. Thanks to the use of satellite and aerial photography and radar, the size and intensity, as well as the speed and direction of approaching hurricanes is now always known well in advance of their arrival. However, to be effective, early-warning systems must be combined with efficient, well-publicised **evacuation routes** so that coastal populations can be hurriedly moved inland. In Miami a set of prescribed hurricane routes lead from the vulnerable shore properties of Miami Beach across the lagoon to Miami which is located on the higher mainland.

The cost of hurricane damage to individuals and families may be offset by **insurance claims**. Similarly, communal damage to schools and other public buildings may be compensated for by State and Federal assistance and emergency **disaster funds**. In these ways localised losses are shared more broadly and subsidised to some extent by the collective body of insurance policy holders and tax-payers generally. None of these financial arrangements minimise the physical damage caused by hurricanes, but they may facilitate rebuilding and speedy recovery.

General Comments

Questions on natural hazards appear with great regularity in the A-level examination. Hazards include those produced by atmospheric conditions such as hurricanes and droughts, tectonic hazards such as earthquakes and volcanic eruptions, geological hazards such as landslides and slope failures, as well as hydrological hazards such as river and coastal flooding. A related subject area concerns human-made disasters such as chemical spills and leakages, oil spills at sea, radioactive contamination, etc. Questions are usually concerned with the perception of risk, monitoring and prediction of the hazard, and strategies for the management and control of hazard impacts.

Related questions

1 (a) What is meant by the term 'environmental perception'? (b) With reference to one specific area, describe how its inhabitants perceive the risk of *either* earthquakes *or* flooding *or* drought.

2 Compare and contrast hurricanes and tornadoes in respect of their causes, characteristics and consequent damage.

3 Is a passive, fatalistic attitude the only realistic response to the threat posed by hurricanes in high-risk areas?

Examine the role of vegetation in coastal development in two of the following habitats: (a) sand dunes; (b) salt-marshes; (c) shingle spits.

Tackling the question

This question is concerned indirectly with the plant succession in two of three different coastal habitats, selected from sand dunes, salt-marshes and shingle spits. Questions in biogeography of this type require quite detailed information about the most common plants associated with different types of habitat. It is not sufficient to write wholly in general terms. You need to refer to specific species, at least by their common names, and ideally by their formal botanical nomenclature.

There is more to this question than just a recital of the typical plant succession in each of your selected habitats. The question is essentially about the role of vegetation as an agent of coastal change. The two processes, plant succession and coastal evolution, are of course inter-related. The best answers will clarify and elucidate those inter-relationships with reference to appropriate locations.

Answer

Each selected habitat is clearly identified with a heading. Don't leave the examiner to guess which parts of the question you have chosen to answer. In the absence of any information about the allocation of marks, you should assume that the two parts of the question carry equal weight. In the sample answer the two parts are of roughly the same length.

(a) Sand dunes

Before considering the role of vegetation in the development of coastal sand dunes, it may be useful to summarise the general conditions which are conducive to dune formation in order to place the biological processes involved in a broader context. Factors which encourage dune formation include prevailing onshore winds blowing across a wide inter-tidal zone which allows the top sand to dry out between tides and to be set in motion by the wind. There should also be some feature at the head of the beach to trap the sand being driven onshore by the wind. This might be patches of coarse shingle or drifted debris or existing vegetation just beyond the high water mark. Ideally, there should be an absence of vegetation on those parts of the beach from which sand is being moved, and active colonisation by plants at the head of the beach where dunes are accumulating. Obviously, not all of these conditions will be met in every area of dune formation, but they indicate the optimum conditions for sand dune accumulation and growth.

The initial accumulation of sand at the head of a beach is often around a clump of coarse grass, such as sea couch grass (*Agropyron junceum*). The next stage, provided that the incipient dune is not destroyed as fast as it accumulates, is the colonisation by marram grass (*Ammophila arenaria*). Marram grass possesses a deep branching system of roots which effectively bind the dune together. Furthermore, the plant itself only survives as long as a fresh supply of sand is constantly added to the dune. Once this supply of fresh sand ceases, the marram will die out and will be replaced by other species of plants. Other characteristic plants at the marram stage include sea-holly (*Eryngium maritimum*), sea spurge (*Euphorbia paralias*), and sea sandwort (*Arenaria pepliodes*). In this early stage, the sand of the dunes has not undergone any particular change, and hence the dunes are sometimes referred to as white dunes.

The supply of sand may be cut off by the accumulation of shingle in front of the developing dune. On this new shingle a further dune may start to form, thus cutting off the supply of sand to the earlier dune. With the reduction of a supply of moving sand, the marram grass will become rather patchy and replaced by lichens, mosses and other plants. At the same time, the decay of earlier plants will start to give a little humus to the sand. If there is shell material in the sand, some solution may take place and lead to the precipitation of carbonate of lime at lower levels. As a result of these developments, the nature of the vegetation changes and a more complex plant cover starts to appear on the dunes. The colour of the sand also changes from white to grey as the dunes grow older.

During the transitional stage from young, white dunes to old, grey dunes there is a great danger of erosion and destruction of the dune system. As the marram grass dies off, and while the replacement vegetation is colonising the sand, there is an incomplete and inadequate plant cover to protect the dunes. Thus, either unaided, or helped by the burrowing of rabbits, burning of the grass or human trampling and other damage, the wind may start to attack the exposed sand. Erosion may be so great as to tear a gap through the dunes, such a feature being described as a **blow-out**. The sand thus eroded accumulates down-wind from the dune, where, being fresh, it is usually quickly re-colonised by marram grass and becomes stabilised. Thus, it is common to see large spreads of this grass in thriving condition at the back of old, grey dunes. Good examples are to be seen on the landward side of the main dunes fronting Scolt Head Island on the North Norfolk coast.

Five plants associated with sand dune habitats are identified in this paragraph.

Some examples of plant species associated with older dune systems could have been mentioned here. Most plants mentioned in the preceding paragraph are typical of young dunes.

Two examples of dune coasts are mentioned by name. You will obviously refer to locations known to you. If you happen to have done fieldwork on sand dune habitats, then it goes without saying that you should refer to that experience.

Dunes may build up to considerable heights. Many contain 15–20 m of sand. Dunes higher than this are nearly always found to be piled up on a foundation of solid rock. For example, dunes at Pennard Burrows in the Gower Peninsula reach a height of 60 m, but have been built up on sloping ground at the head of the beach. However, whatever their size and complexity, vegetation inevitably plays an important role in the initial formation, subsequent growth and stabilisation of all coastal dune systems.

(b) Salt-marshes

Salt-marshes consist of broad, flat, low-lying expanses of silt and mud deposited by the sea in the sheltered waters of bays and estuaries or on the landward side of spits and bars. Although areas of salt-marsh normally support a complex, dendritic system of tidal creeks, and also have small patches of open water on their surface (salt pans), most of their surface is normally covered by a distinctive assemblage of salt-loving plants. Indeed, these plants play a crucial role in both the initial formation and subsequent development of salt-marsh areas.

Evidence of background reading is provided in both this and the following paragraph, with references to the work of Sparks and the classic text on British coastal geomorphology by J.A. Steers.

The development of coastal marshes has been summarised by B.W. Sparks. He notes that any foreshore of gentle gradient can be seen to possess irregularities on its surface, usually in the form of broad ridges and shallow depressions. When such areas are gently flooded by the tide, fine sediment carried in suspension will be deposited over the whole foreshore. However, owing to the fact that ebbing tidal water is confined to the depressions, sediment does not accumulate there to the same extent as on the ridges. Sediment accumulation on the ridges is aided by seaweed and flotsam which hinder the flow of the tide and further encourage deposition. Eventually, when sufficient deposition has occurred, the higher parts of the foreshore will be colonised by vegetation.

As in the previous section on sand dunes, reference is made to some of the most common salt-marsh plant species. In this case, eight species are mentioned by name. If you don't have this level of detailed information, then this question, and others of this type, are probably best left alone.

The role of salt-loving or **halophytic plants** in salt-marsh development has been examined by J.A. Steers who made a close study of the coastal marshes of North Norfolk. He noted that early colonisers of silt and mud banks in that area include marsh samphire (*Salicornia spp.*) and herbaceous sea blite (*Suaeda maritima*). Neither of these plants develops a very thick cover and in winter they are reduced to bare stalks, so that they alone would hardly provide a trap for further sediment. However, they frequently have seaweed entangled in their stems, and in that way check water movement and encourage further sedimentation. In this way the surface of the marsh will grow slowly upwards. Measurements of accretion rates carried out by Steers on the salt marshes of Scolt Head Island in North Norfolk and on the Dyfi marshes of West Wales showed that accretion is rapid on the low marshes which are covered by every tide, becomes even more rapid once a close cover of plants has been established, and then slows down on the higher marshes which are inundated less frequently by the tide.

With continued deposition and upward growth of salt marshes, the plant cover changes. The distribution of particular species is closely related to the frequency and duration of tidal inundation on different parts of the marsh. As mentioned above, the lowest parts of the marsh which are covered with water for the longest period each day are characterised by *Salicornia spp.* and *Suaeda maritima*. At higher levels, sea aster (*Aster tripolium*) and common marsh grass (*Pucinellia maritima*) begin to appear. Higher still, one finds sea pink (*Armeria maritima*), sand spurrey (*Spergularia media*) and sea lavender (*Limonium humile*). At the head of the marsh, around its landward margin, clumps of shrubby sea blite (*Suaeda fruticosa*) are typical. However, the sequence of plant colonies varies in detail from one area of salt-marsh to another. Steers, for example, recorded striking differences between the coastal marshes of the east and west coasts of England and Wales.

Two relatively minor features of salt-marsh areas should also be mentioned; namely, tidal creeks and salt pans. During the early stages of marsh formation, areas of non-deposition (the original foreshore depressions) are converted into **tidal creeks**. In this way, the ebb and flow of the tide becomes concentrated along these lines and colonisation by plants is prevented by tidal scour. **Salt pans** are small, roughly circular pools on the surface of the marsh. The suggestion has been made that the very high salinity of the water contained in these pools inhibits plant colonisation and resultant infilling. Finally, mention should be made of the human influence on salt-marsh habitats. Once a marsh has built up to such a level that it is seldom covered by tides, it is relatively simple to enclose it with a bank or wall, drain it, and replace the natural vegetation with cultivated pasture. Obviously, at that ultimate stage in salt-marsh development, the plant cover is almost wholly a result of human interference rather than a response to natural conditions.

General Comments

In very general terms, questions in biogeography can be divided into two broad categories. Firstly, there are those which are concerned with ecosystems at macro-scale, such as the characteristics and distribution of global vegetation systems; for example, Tropical Rain Forest, Tropical Grasslands, Northern Coniferous Forests, Tundra, etc. Secondly, there are questions which focus on ecosystems at micro-scale, such as detailed, localised studies of, for example, dune or salt-marsh habitats. Questions in the second category are usually concerned with the interactions and inter-relationships between the component parts of the ecosystem, and also with the effects of human activity.

Related questions

1 With reference to heathland habitats, describe and explain the inter-relationships that exist between the main components.

2 With reference to examples, discuss the proposition that 'the diversity and complexity of any plant habitat increases with age'.

3 Describe how you might carry out a survey of the distribution of plant species on a small area of coastal dunes or salt-marshes.

Question 14

Describe the causes and consequences of *either*
atmospheric pollution *or* river pollution.

Tackling the question

The wording of the question is such that you may choose either one of two themes for your answer — atmospheric pollution or river pollution. Make sure that you identify your choice at the beginning of the answer. The examiner will not want to read half a page or more before he or she is certain of your choice. The question sets two tasks: description of causes, and description of consequences. You could organise the answer in two different ways: either deal with all the causes first and then follow that with a description of all the consequences; or deal with causes and consequences in parallel, describing each type of cause and its related consequences, paragraph by paragraph. This answer uses the first approach. Either essay plan would be equally acceptable.

Material on pollution can be quite technical. Make sure that you understand the chemical and biological process involved in river pollution, and feel confident that you can use the technical terminology precisely and correctly. If not, this might be a topic area to avoid.

Answer

River pollution

One of the basic problems in any discussion of water pollution concerns terminology. There are many types of water pollution and many types of pollutants, so that it is not always clear whether descriptions of pollution in different rivers and catchments are referring to like, or even similar, conditions. River pollution can be described and measured in terms of turbidity, oxygen deficiency, mineral content, the presence of toxins, temperature modifications, radioactivity, and, of course, biological disruption of the aquatic ecosystem. In very broad terms, a river may be said to be polluted when the water in it is adversely altered in composition or condition, directly or indirectly, as a result of human activity. A pollutant can be defined as a substance or effect which damages the environment by changing

Guidance notes

Provide a simple identification to show which part of the question you are answering.

The first two paragraphs constitute the introduction. They contain simple definitions of 'pollution' and 'pollutant', and mention methods and problems of measurement and the limitations of the data available.

the growth rate of species, interferes with food chains, is toxic, or interferes with the health and amenities of people.

Pollution is most commonly expressed in terms of **biological oxygen demand** (BOD). This is the amount of oxygen in milligrams per litre (mg/l) consumed within a water sample over 5 days at 20°C in a dark enclosed container. This indicates the potential de-oxygenation of water due to the presence of organic pollutants. It does not, of course, provide any information about pollution from chemical toxins or radioactive nuclides or micro-organisms. Published data should also be treated with caution. Levels of pollution vary over time in relation to the flood hydrograph. High water-levels dilute pollutants; low levels increase their concentration. Sources of river pollution can be divided into three broad categories — industrial, agricultural and domestic — and these will be described in turn.

The section on causes of pollution starts here. It is arranged by sources of pollution — industrial, agricultural and domestic.

Most **industrial waste** is in the form of **effluent** which can be defined as any solid, liquid or gaseous product, in treated or untreated condition, which is discharged from an industrial process. Industrial effluent includes organic solvents, suspended solids, dissolved chemical compounds, oils, etc. It varies in strength from dirty water to highly toxic metallic and organic sludge. Industrial effluent may be treated by the producer, or fed into sewers and treated as sewage. Some, illegally in the UK, is still fed directly into rivers and estuaries. Industrial treatment of effluent by its producers usually involves the separation of suspended solid and dissolved substances from the liquid base. The latter is then fed into sewers or rivers, while the former, usually in the form of sludge, is disposed of by tipping on waste disposal sites. Industrial sludge may contain highly toxic compounds, which can enter the ground water and eventually reach rivers and streams. The total amount of industrial effluent discharged directly into the rivers of England and Wales has been estimated at about 12 million m³ per year.

Notice how examples are worked into the answer. You will need to learn similar examples for use in examination essays.

Another form of river pollution related to industrial activity concerns the discharge of warm water into rivers, notably from power stations. This is referred to as **thermal pollution**. For example, below the Iron Bridge power station, the River Severn undergoes a temperature increase of between 0.5°C and 0.8°C depending on the volume of discharge. Other causes of industrial pollution of rivers and estuaries include accidental spillage of oil and chemicals during transit and accidental leakage from industrial storage tanks adjacent to rivers. In 1969, drums containing 100 kg of the insecticide Endosulfan rolled off a barge into the River Rhine, polluting the river downstream for more than 100 km and killing thousands of fish.

Modern **agricultural activities** constitute another important source of river pollution. Factory farming, involving the rearing of cattle, pigs and poultry in buildings, produces enormous amounts of **manure slurry**. Another highly toxic agricultural waste is the effluent from silos used for silage production. Farmers are not permitted to discharge these materials directly into rivers, and most is sprayed onto arable land or grassland. An estimated 60 million m³ of manure slurry is disposed of in this way each year in England and Wales. Many of the constituents of this waste find their way, via surface run-off and seepage, into water courses. The growing use of highly toxic **chemical pesticides and herbicides** is another source of water pollution, as is the widespread use of **nitrogenous and phosphatic fertilisers**. The effect may be gauged from the fact that the River Thames contained five times as much nitrate in 1977 as in 1948.

The main **domestic source** of river pollution is **sewage effluent**. This is usually treated at sewage works by sedimentation and biological filtration processes before being discharged into rivers, although large quantities of untreated sewage are still discharged into estuaries and coastal waters. An estimated 10 million m³ of sewage effluent is discharged into the rivers of England and Wales each year, of which 14% is untreated or, at best, receives only cursory primary treatment. However, even treated sewage may not conform to the minimum standard laid down as long ago as 1912 by the Royal Commission on Sewage Disposal. One reason for this is that many sewage works are old and obsolete and are now working far beyond their original planned capacity. They are also receiving materials for which they were never designed, such as 'hard' synthetic detergents which are not readily biodegradable. A variety of toxic industrial waste may also pass untreated through conventional sewage works. Sewage treatment produces large quantities of waste sludge, most of which is either dumped at sea or used as landfill. This latter process, together with **domestic refuse dumping**, may contaminate ground water supplies with heavy metals and other toxins, and lead to pollution of streams and rivers.

The **consequences** of river pollution are extremely varied and, in many cases, interrelated. Physical effects include the presence of suspended solids. These will either settle out or remain in suspension. Particles which settle out will accumulate on vegetation and form deposits on the river-bed. Their effect is to cause **reduced photosynthesis** and **oxygen depletion**. Water polluted with organic waste, such as sewage, will experience drastic oxygen depletion because organic material requires oxygen for its decomposition. Particles which remain in suspension cause **increased turbidity, reduced light penetration and restricted plant growth**. Suspended particles may clog the gill surfaces of fish and interfere with filter feeders. Silting

The section on consequences of pollution starts here. Because the consequences are inter-related they are less easy to classify than the causes of pollution. Separate paragraphs have been used to describe physical effects, chemical toxic effects, chemical nutrient effects and human health hazards.

may also cause **destruction of spawning grounds** of trout and salmon by preventing the development of eggs. Because most aquatic plants can only exist within a narrow temperature range, thermal pollution will kill off many species of plants and fish and cause **radical changes in the species structure of the aquatic ecosystem**.

Pollution may involve **chemical toxic effects** as a result of concentrations of heavy metals (mercury, lead, copper, zinc, arsenic, etc.), salts, acids, alkalis, and other organic compounds such as phenols and cyanides. Accumulation of these pollutants in tissues may be lethal for many species. Chemical pesticides, such as DDT, are known to be particularly hazardous. Toxins may build up in food chains and even affect human populations. At Toyama in Japan, industrial waste containing cadmium was discharged into the River Jintsh, and more than 100 people died as a result of eating fish from the river.

River pollution commonly produces **chemical nutrient effects**. Water may become excessively enriched with nutrients. These may be either organic (derived from sewage) or inorganic (derived from inorganic fertilisers). Increased chemical nutrients encourage dense, slimy, surface growths of algae which reduce light penetration and reduce oxygenation of the water. Again, this alters food chains, kills most fish, and causes complete **disruption of the ecosystem**. This process, known as **eutrophication**, is particularly common in lakes (e.g. Lough Neagh in Northern Ireland). There is also growing concern about the quality of drinking water extracted from rivers with high concentrations of nitrates. Nitrates taken into the body can cause disease and may even be a cause of stomach cancer.

River basins may also become polluted with **micro-organisms**, which also constitute a serious **health hazard** for humans. Many bacteria are water-borne, including those responsible for cholera, typhoid, dysentery and gastro-enteritis; similarly, water-borne viruses include those causing hepatitis and salmonella infections. The infective egg and laval stages of round-worms and tape-worms are also found in water. All of these micro-organisms are present in sewage and farm slurry. Most are removed by sewage treatment, but not all; some enter rivers in sewage effluent and others find their way into water courses by seepage and percolation of manure slurry spread onto the land.

River pollution is a serious problem. In recent years there has been a growing awareness of the issues involved but, at the same time, continued urbanisation and industrialisation and the continued growth of population produce ever-increasing amounts of waste for disposal. In Britain, legislation such as the Water Resources Act (1963) and the Control of Pollution Act (1974) have led to some improvements, notably in the

Thames catchment area. But, while some rivers have improved, others have deteriorated, and the condition of heavily polluted rivers (such as the Tyne, Wear, Tees, Trent, and Mersey) remains a national disgrace.

The conclusion takes the form of a brief review of the present state of Britain's rivers.

General Comments

This is one of several questions in the book dealing with human impacts on the natural environment. (See also Questions 10, 11, 15, 17 and 18.) With the growing concern about the 'costs' of development expressed in terms of environmental damage, and with the increasing awareness of 'green' issues, this has become an important field of study in recent years. An understanding of topics such as environmental damage, environmental protection and environmental management policies should be an important part of your exam preparation. Questions on these issues may appear in either the physical or human sections of the exam.

Related questions

1   What is meant by the term 'eutrophication'? With reference to examples, describe the causes and consequences of the process.

2   Discuss the view that pollution is an inevitable consequence of economic progress.

3   To what extent should river pollution be regarded as an urban problem?

Question 15

Examine the impacts of human activity on coastal change.

Tackling the question

This is one of several questions in the book which require you to examine the impacts of human activity on the natural environment. In this case the focus is on coastal impacts. In general terms it is possible to distinguish between intentional, planned changes on the shoreline, and unintentional, unplanned, unforeseen effects of human activity on coastal morphology. Thus, in organising the answer, these two broad themes lie at the heart of the essay plan.

This is a very 'open' question. Many different types and scales of human activity could justifiably be included, from, for example, massive reclamation schemes to very localised trampling of vegetation on sand dunes. Nor is the question tied to any particular location. With such 'open' questions, it is often advisable to make the answer as focused as possible by referring to actual processes in actual areas. Case studies and examples are especially important. The sample answer makes reference to a dozen different locations where human activity has caused coastal modifications. Some are simply mentioned in passing, others examined in more detail. You should aim to match that in your own answer.

Answer

This is a rather long introductory paragraph which places human activity along coasts into a general context. It also serves to introduce the distinction between direct and indirect effects, a point which is picked up in the next paragraph.

Coastal regions are among the most continually changing zones on the earth's surface. Enormous forces are at work, generated by wave action and the movement of water by tides and currents. Placed in that context, the impacts of human activity are very small indeed. On the other hand, examined at a more localised and detailed level, their effects may be considerable. Much depends on the scale of investigation. Understandably, human activity has not been a very effective agent of change along high energy coasts, and has had far greater impact in producing change and modifying natural processes along prograding, outbuilding shorelines of low coastal energy. As a further general point, it should be mentioned that the inhabitants of coastal areas have encountered a slow, imperceptible rise of sea-level during the post-glacial period. 'Without being aware of it, man has been combatting the eustatic rise of sea-level in many areas. This recent period of rise of the sea and its resultant slow invasion of the land should also be taken into consideration when estimating the long-term effects of man on coastal change.' (J.H. Davis) The influence of human activity on geomorphological change in coastal areas may be considered under two broad headings; **direct influences** which are planned and intentional, and **indirect influences** which, in many cases, are unintentional and often unforeseen. Both types of change may be either positive (beneficial) or negative (detrimental). They will be considered in turn.

Coastal areas have long exercised a strong attraction for settlement, trade, leisure and recreation. Thus, the growth of coastal activity may be related to increasing population pressure in many areas. The **direct influences** of human activity on coastlines include major **civil engineering** works, such as the development of ports and harbours, the construction of quays and jetties, the building of piers and promenades, the dredging and enlargement of shipping channels and, most spectacular of all, the **reclamation** of land from beneath the sea. No better example of this latter process can be found than in the Netherlands, where the draining and reclamation of the former Zuider Zee represents the most ambitious project of its kind ever undertaken. The draining of the Zuider Zee began in 1927 according to a plan devised by the hydraulic engineer, Cornelis Lely. The scheme involved the construction of a 30 km-long enclosing dam across the northern end of the Zuider Zee to create a vast freshwater lake, the Ijsselmeer, from which four polders have been reclaimed to date. Not only has the scheme added 165,000 ha of valuable land to a small and overcrowded nation, but it has also reduced the length of the Dutch coastline by 300 km, thereby eliminating the risk of sea floods along what had previously been a very vulnerable coast subject to frequent devastating floods.

As a further example of the human influence on coasts, but on a much smaller scale, mention might be made of attempts at **foreshore protection** by the construction of various types of sea-wall and other coastal defences. The aim is to protect beaches, dunes and low sandy cliffs from excessive erosion. Success in this respect has been limited, and in many cases unexpected and indirect results have occurred. It has been noted that 'too many of the things done to improve and protect beach-fronting property have actually had the effect of accelerating erosion or transferring the problem elsewhere' (W.V. Williams). Simple **earth banks** may be used along tidal creeks and estuaries and other sheltered sections of coast. During severe storms, such banks may be overtopped or breached as a result of weaknesses resulting from seepage. This occurred along parts of the Essex coast during the East Coast flood disaster of 1953.

Because it is such an outstanding example of coastal modification, this example is described in some detail.

Much smaller scale changes, such as the building of defensive banks and walls, are brought in next. Attention is drawn to the fact that these have often produced unintended results.

Attempts to reduce longshore drift are mentioned next. Two examples of unforeseen consequences are mentioned in the concluding sentence of the paragraph.

The theme of this paragraph, replacement and removal of beach material, is presented wholly by means of examples. This can be quite effective, but should not be overdone. The recommended style for geographical writing is a balanced mixture of broad general statements and supportive factual material.

Sea-walls of stone or concrete are more effective. However, various studies have shown that waves tend to rise higher on sea-walls, whether of the stepped or smooth-faced concave type, and thus fall with greater force at the base of the wall, and may, as a result, actually increase beach scour and accelerate erosion and lowering of the beach at the foot of the wall. Alternatively, destructive wave action may be transmitted in a down-wave direction to adjacent areas lacking sea-wall protection.

Where loss of beach material by longshore drifting is a serious local problem, attempts may be made to trap material by means of **groynes** or breakwaters. These are usually of timber or concrete construction, the most effective ones being those which can be raised by additional sections to keep pace with beach accumulation. Model studies of groynes by the Hydraulics Research Board have suggested that the length, orientation and spacing of groynes must be carefully related to beach characteristics and the nature of the longshore drift process in any area. As a general rule, groynes should be spaced at an interval roughly equivalent to their length in order to produce the best results. It has been shown that groynes 3 m high and 60 m long at 60 m intervals can reduce the loss of beach material to as little as one-eighth of the original value. Long low groynes appear to be more effective traps than high structures closely spaced. However, it is well-known that success in one area can cause serious problems elsewhere. Beaches in a down-wave direction may become starved of material and suffer severe erosion as a result. The building of a breakwater at Newhaven caused erosion at nearby Seaford, and the construction of a pier at Gorleston led to erosion at Lowestoft.

The **replacement of beach material** is another technique of foreshore protection which has been used in some areas. For example, at Port Huemene in California, two jetties built out from the mainland caused accretion on the up-wave side and rapid erosion on the down-wave side. The technique employed was to dredge beach material from the up-wave side of the jetties and transfer it to the eroded beach on the down-wave side in an attempt to regain stability. **Removal of beach material** is sometimes carried out, usually with disastrous results. A well-known example is that of Hallsands in Devon where 660,000 tonnes of shingle were removed for use in the construction of the naval dockyards at nearby Plymouth. This reduced the level of the beach by about 4 m. The shingle was not replaced naturally and cliff erosion at the head of the beach followed — about 6 m of recession between 1907 and 1957. As a result, the village of Hallsands has been subject to wave attack and is now mostly abandoned and in ruins.

Another type of coastal environment which is particularly susceptible to human interference is that of young, unstable dune formations. Dunes near coastal resorts are particularly vulnerable to damage from trampling and the destruction of vegetation. Techniques of **dune protection** include the use of brushwood fencing to encourage sand accumulation, the planting of marram grass, the establishment of plantations of conifers, and restriction on public access. All of these techniques have been applied to dune coasts in the Netherlands, along the Baltic coast of North Germany, and in the dunes of Les Landes on the Atlantic coast of France. In all cases, careful management has done much to improve dune stability and reduce the risk of blow-outs.

The **indirect influences** of human activity on coastlines are more difficult to evaluate. In many cases, they are integrated with, or obscured by, natural processes so that measurement is impossible. Often they are the result of **activities inland**. For example, deforestation and agricultural malpractices may lead to soil erosion, which in turn may lead to estuarine sedimentation and coastal progradation. It has been suggested that the rate of growth of the Tigris–Euphrates delta can be related to the efficiency and maintenance of inland canal and irrigation systems. In North America, the growth of the Mississippi delta has almost certainly accelerated since the arrival of Europeans in North America. In other words, artificially induced changes in the sediment load of rivers will affect the sediment budget of shorelines and their movement over a period of time.

Pollution of coastal waters can also produce serious changes in coastal ecology. Delicate states of balance are easily upset by human interference, whether intentional or unforeseen. For example, in the Dry Tortugas island group near Key West in Florida, the protection of bird life led to increased numbers; this in turn led to a loss of vegetation which had hitherto checked erosion; as a result, erosion increased, eventually causing the complete destruction of one small island in the group. Along parts of Long Island Sound, the pollution of bays has led to the growth of blooms of plankton and algae which have had the effect of reducing wave energy which, in turn, has led to increased rates of silting and sedimentation.

During the present century, it has become obvious that human activity is capable of producing enormous changes to the natural environment. The scale of those changes may be related to both the accelerating growth of world population and the technological developments which have provided the means to effect massive changes. Some changes have been planned and deliberate, others inadvertent. However, it is increasingly clear that even the best intentioned changes may trigger off a complex chain of events, and that coastal areas require particularly careful and sensitive management.

The management and control of sand dune habitats is the final theme in this section of the answer which deals with direct human intervention.

The final section of the essay is devoted to indirect human impacts on coastal change. The treatment is inevitably broad and general, although some attempt has been made to introduce appropriate examples of the processes at work.

This is a very conventional conclusion; a simple summary of the key themes identified in the essay.

General Comments

In general terms, questions on coastal geomorphology are of two types. Firstly, there are rather traditional questions which are designed to test your understanding of coastal processes (erosion, transportation and deposition) and the resultant landforms (cliffs, beaches, spits and bars, etc.). These are relatively easy questions. Increasingly, a second category of questions is becoming more important. These are questions which are concerned with the effects of human activity on the type and rate of shoreline processes. This second category also includes questions on coastal management, including themes such as coastal protection, beach and dune stabilisation, salt-marsh reclamation, etc.

Related questions

1 Describe and evaluate the various techniques which have been designed to combat the problems of coastal erosion.

2 With reference to a range of examples, discuss the impacts of industrial development on estuaries in the UK.

3 Examine the consequences of the practice of dumping industrial waste and sewage at sea.

Question 16

Examine the constraints on human activity imposed by the climate of *either* Arctic *or* Equatorial regions.

Tackling the question

This question requires you to examine the constraints on human activity imposed by either one of two extreme climatic regimes. The context for this examination is the long-standing debate among geographers about geographical determinism and geographical possibilism; that is to say, the extent to which population is controlled by or exercises control over the physical environment. In the case of extreme environments, such as those specified in the question, the truth probably lies somewhere between the two extreme debating positions. Clearly, climate does impose some constraints, but population in such areas also displays physiological and cultural adaptations, and new technologies bring new freedoms and options.

From these first thoughts an essay plan starts to emerge. The climate regime needs to be described, and the constraints on human activity have to be identified. But the essay must also include reference to adaptations and acclimatisation, and, of course, the impact of late twentieth-century technology.

Answer

Guidance notes

> Identify at the outset which of the two options you have selected to answer.

> The first paragraph is concerned with defining the climatic type which forms the subject of the essay.

Arctic regions: climatic constraints

If the term 'Arctic' is defined in the strictest sense to mean the area north of the Arctic Circle (latitude 66.5°N), it is found to contain two climatic types: a belt of sub-Arctic climate in the south, and a belt of polar climate in the north. These are the Dc and the Dd climates (sub-Arctic) and the ET and EF climates (tundra and ice cap) in the Köppen and Trewartha systems of climate classification. The sub-Arctic type of climate is characterised by short, warm summers and long cold winters. Precipitation is light to moderate, mostly in the form of snow in winter. Further north, the polar climate is characterised by very short, cool summers (only 2–4 months above freezing) and long, bitterly cold winters. Precipitation is generally light, much of it in the form of snow. The boundary between the sub-Arctic and polar types of climate is usually taken as the July 10°C isotherm. That is to say, mean summer temperatures in the polar climate zone fail to reach 10°C, whereas the sub-Arctic climate zone enjoys a brief summer period with mean summer temperatures rising above 10°C. The same isotherm also corresponds very closely with the boundary between **tundra** and **taiga** habitats, and the boundary between continuous and discontinuous permafrost. Examples of the two types of climate are given below.

Climatic station	Latitude	January mean	July mean	Precipitation	Type
Gällivare, Sweden	67°N	–11°C	15°C	560 mm	Dc
Ruskoye Ust'ye, Russia	71°N	–39°C	9°C	142 mm	ET

The characteristics of the climate regime are described in this paragraph. Make sure to mention all the relevant problems and constraints.

High latitude environments have been described as 'areas of human stress'. Inhabitants of the Far North are subject to a number of severe environmental constraints, some a direct consequence of climate, others only indirectly related to climate and high latitude position. The most obvious constraint is that of the **intense winter cold**. Extremely low temperatures are often combined with **fierce winds**, a characteristic feature of the treeless tundra with its lack of shelter and wind breaks. Severe **wind chill** makes winter conditions even worse than temperature statistics alone might suggest. The fact that life is lived on a cover of **snow and ice** for much of the year also imposes further constraints on movement and activity. Areas north of the Arctic Circle also experience marked seasonal variations in the length of day and night. In winter, there is a period of **continuous darkness** when the sun fails to rise above the horizon, and in summer a corresponding period of **continuous daylight** when the sun never drops below the horizon. The duration of these periods of continuous daylight and darkness lengthens with increasing distance north of the Arctic Circle. At latitude 80°N, there are 15 weeks of continuous daylight in summer. Another environmental constraint in the Northlands relates to the low biological productivity of the tundra ecosystem, which is characterised by low species diversity and slow rates of replacement. That is a direct consequence of the brief growing season and the climatic regime of these high latitude areas.

It has been remarked that 'man is in many respects a tropical animal, and it is reasonable to ask whether he can live in the

Far North' (G.M. Brown). The answer to that question is yes — but only if he is willing to pay the price. That price is impossible to quantify in purely monetary or economic terms, but rather should be thought of in terms of the constraints on 'normal' human activity. It involves the need to create a microclimate in order to survive (special clothing and shelters), reduced mobility, diminished dexterity, enforced idleness for long periods, isolation and loneliness, lack of amenities, the discomfort of intense cold, and the risk of actual physical damage and injury (frostbite). Measured in those terms, the price of living in the Far North is a very high one indeed. On the other hand, people are by no means passive and powerless, and are capable of responding and adapting to their surroundings. Those **adaptations** are both **physiological** (physical) and **cultural** (social).

In recent years, many studies have been carried out on the extent to which the indigenous populations of high latitudes are able to acclimatise to cold conditions. Much of this work has involved clinical tests on Inuit (Eskimo) groups in North America, and the comparison of results with those for the non-acclimatised (newly-arrived) population in the North. The processes of body temperature regulation are highly complicated, but one recent study reported that 'there are significant physiological differences between acclimatised and non-acclimatised populations'. Cultural adaptations to cold may also be noted among the Inuit. These include clothing which is carefully adapted to conditions of extreme cold. Likewise, traditional shelters such as the igloo and tupik, and modern permanent buildings, are carefully designed to offer both a high degree of insulation against cold and good circulation of air. Diet also helps. The Inuit require 4,000–5,000 calories per day to keep warm and carry out strenuous activities. That is provided by a diet of fish and meat (seal, walrus and caribou) which is rich in fat and protein and low in carbohydrate.

For the inhabitants of high latitude areas, the daily round of work and domestic activity is carried out on a cover of snow and ice. For most of the year, the environment is one of snow, pack-ice and ice-floes, all of which present a high level of **danger and hazard**, and a high risk of serious accident. The dangers are from falls, over-exposure to snow and blizzards, immersion in freezing water, and so on. The response to these dangers is largely cultural, and involves education from elders about subtle variations in snow and ice conditions and impending changes in the weather. Most activities, for example hunting, are undertaken collectively in groups rather than individually. This enhances survival chances in the event of accident. Nevertheless, despite these social responses, the physical constraints of an environment of snow and ice on movement and activity are still considerable.

The determinist/possibilist debate starts to emerge in this paragraph, although that terminology is not actually used.

Acclimatisation and adaptation are discussed in this and the following paragraph.

The way in which technology can provide an insulating barrier from the climatic environment is introduced here. Mention is also made of the high cost of such technology. The example of the oil-company worker at Prudhoe Bay is a good one, especially in an answer which is rather 'thin' on examples and references to specific Arctic locations.

The periods of continuous winter darkness and summer daylight experienced within the Arctic appear to have a disruptive effect on sleep-wakefulness patterns as well as work and domestic routines. In particular, the lack of sunlight in winter, combined with the intense cold, appears to be most disruptive, and in its worst manifestations can produce mental stress and disorientation. Various writers have described symptoms of depression, melancholia, lethargy and memory loss during the long, gloomy Arctic winter. This condition is referred to as 'cabin fever' in Alaska and Yukon, and 'mörkesyk' (literally dark-sickness) in Arctic Norway. Newcomers to the North appear to be worst affected, and many find winter conditions intolerable. Thus, Arctic mining companies and other enterprises not only have trouble in recruiting labour, but also suffer from a high turn-over of workers and a lack of stability of the workforce.

It might be supposed that the constraints imposed by climate have been largely relaxed by modern **technology**. To some extent that is true. The geophysicist working at Prudhoe Bay on the North Slope of Alaska enjoys the comfort of brightly-lit, well-heated, efficiently-insulated living quarters; he watches TV, enjoys a meal of fresh food flown in from the south, telephones his family in Los Angeles, and may be unaware of the Arctic blizzard which rages outside the base. This is a lifestyle which bears no comparison with that of, say, a nineteenth-century fur-trapper or gold prospector in the same area. Nor indeed, does it bear comparison with the hardship and deprivation still endured by many of those who inhabit the Northlands at the present time. Technology can help, but, as always, the cost is high. Buildings require special foundations, double and triple glazing, additional insulation and heating; waste disposal poses special problems. Service pipes and pipelines have to be raised above the ground because of the permafrost; roads and airstrips require elaborate foundations for the same reason. All of this is very costly and, even with all the benefits of twentieth-century technology, people are still constrained by the Arctic climate to a very considerable degree. Geographical determinism, whereby human activities are thought to be controlled and influenced by the environment, has long been unfashionable and largely discredited. In the Arctic, in this most demanding and punishing of environments, it would still appear to have some relevance.

Relationships between population and environment lie at the heart of every A-level geography syllabus. In recent years this has become a clear focus for the subject. Large numbers of questions seek to demonstrate the links between the 'physical' and 'human' sides of the subject and to show the holistic, integrated nature of geography. However, examination of questions set on that relationship shows that most are concerned with human impacts on the environment, and relatively few with the converse aspect of the relationship; namely, the constraints on human activity posed by the environment. That side of the relationship is rarely questioned. Thus, this question is the only one in the collection which explores the influence of the environment, in this case climate, on human activity.

Related questions

1   Discuss the problems of resource development in high latitude regions.

2   Examine the proposition that high latitude areas can never support more than a very small, scattered, low-density population.

3   With reference to examples, explain why certain regions of the world still remain as largely unspoilt wilderness areas. Comment on the importance of such areas in a global context.

(a) **What were the reasons for the establishment of the various National Parks in Britain? (5 marks)**

(b) **Large numbers of visitors to National Parks can create serious environmental problems. Briefly describe the nature of such problems. (10 marks)**

(c) **Describe the possible strategies which might be employed to deal with any one of the problems identified above. (10 marks)**

Tackling the question

This is a three-part question with clearly designated sections and a specified allocation of marks for each one. Other examples of this type of question are found elsewhere in the book (see Questions 11, 12 and 18). It is becoming increasingly common for examiners to indicate the weighting given to each section of this type of 'part-question'. By implication, sections (b) and (c) should contain substantially more material (concepts, facts, examples, etc.) than section (a) which carries only half the marks allocated to the other two sections. The answers to sections (b) and (c) are likely to be longer than the answer to section (a), although not necessarily so. The whole point about weighted questions is to do with your allocation of time in the examination. Clearly, there is little point in spending an excessive amount of time on an answer which, at best, can earn very few marks. Concentrate on the sections which potentially provide the biggest 'pay-off'.

With this type of divided question there is no requirement to make links or connections between the various parts. Think of each question answer as quite discrete. Make sure that you include the notation of the various sections in your answer. The examiner should not have to search around to discover where section (b) starts and finishes.

Answer

Introducing a topic with a quotation can make a strong and effective opening to an answer, but the answer could start with the second sentence of the second paragraph. After all, the question is only worth five marks.

(a) 'The National Parks are the most beautiful parts of England and Wales. There are many other areas of outstanding natural beauty but none more beautiful. That is why the National Parks were chosen. They are neither state-owned, nor fenced off. They are an inheritance not an invention. And they are there to be enjoyed.' (Brian Redhead, former President of the Council for National Parks, 1988)

This statement by the late Brian Redhead hints at some of the reasons why a series of National Parks were established in Britain during the early postwar years. The aim of the **1949 National Parks and Access to the Countryside Act**, which led to the designation of ten National Parks between 1951 and 1957, was to preserve and enhance some of the most beautiful natural landscapes in Britain, to facilitate public access to those areas, and to encourage their use for leisure and recreation.

The upland districts of England and Wales had long provided a means of escape to the countryside for workers living in the grim industrial and mining towns of nineteenth-century Britain. In the early twentieth century, rambling and hiking had become popular leisure activities, and 'freedom of the hills' was an important campaign in the 1930s, typified by a mass trespass on the grouse moors of Kinder Scout in the Peak District in 1932. In 1936 the Joint Standing Committee for National Parks was set up, and soon after the war various reports on the subject were published, including those by John Dower and Sir Arthur Hobhouse. The 1949 National Parks Act was, therefore, the culmination of a long campaign for the right of public access to the mountains and moorlands of upland Britain.

> Lots of good factual detail here — key names and dates. This type of concise, informative writing really earns the marks.

(b) The growth in private car ownership during the postwar period, together with the expansion of the motorway network, have combined to make the National Parks increasingly accessible for more and more people. For example, the Peak District National Park is now within a three-hour drive for over 25 million people. Even peripheral parks such as Dartmoor and the Brecon Beacons can be reached in well under four hours from London by motorway. Improved and extended accessibility, combined with other factors such as a growth of population, longer holidays, increased leisure time, and a growing interest in the natural environment, have led to a steady increase in the number of visitors to the National Parks. Currently, almost 100 million people visit the National Parks each year. This creates many problems; some social, some economic, and others environmental. It is this latter category which will be considered below.

Visitors tend to concentrate in particular areas or locations within the National Parks. These so-called '**honeypots**' are usually areas of particularly attractive scenery or with important historical or cultural associations. Examples include Malham Cove in the Yorkshire Dales and Hadrian's Wall in the Northumberland Park. Thus, the environmental impacts of visitors tend to be concentrated in particular areas or along particular routes, while other areas may be little affected.

> Good use of examples. You, of course, will refer to locations which you know personally or have studied in class.

Environmental problems caused by large numbers of visitors can be divided into two broad categories. First, there are those which relate to **environmental quality**. These include the **loss of visual amenity** due to the building of car parks, caravan sites, cafes, restaurants, garages, visitor centres and other intrusive elements all designed to cater for the needs of tourists. Related problems include those of litter, vandalism, graffiti, noise and traffic congestion. Secondly, there are **ecological changes** resulting from footpath erosion, vegetation trampling, occurrence of fires and burning of vegetation, removal of rare plant species, disturbance of breeding grounds and natural habitats for birds and animals. All of these problems represent the cost of the principle of right of public access to Britain's scenic uplands and coasts.

(c) Selected problem: footpath erosion

The concentration of visitors along particular routes has led to severe erosion of many paths and tracks. Some of these are long-distance trails, others are paths leading to mountain summits, while others are simply paths leading from a car park to an adjacent vantage point. A 1986 survey in the Three Peaks area of the Yorkshire Dales National Park revealed that of the 65 km of paths, one-third were severely damaged and in need of immediate repair, while a further third were seriously deteriorated. To the south, in the Peak District National Park, parts of the Pennine Way have been eroded down more than a metre below the surface of the local peat cover. Another report estimated that £1.5 million is needed to repair paths on Snowdon along which more than 400,000 people climb to the summit each year. On Dartmoor, paths linking car parks with adjacent tors now form ugly scars across the landscape.

Eroded paths act as channels for the surface flow of rain, and soon turn into quagmires. Walkers, seeking a mud-free path, then start to erode areas adjacent to the original path, so that the natural vegetation may be destroyed over a width of 10 m or more. In extreme cases both the top-soil and sub-soil are washed away to leave boulder-filled gullies.

The solution to these problems usually requires the formulation of a **management plan**. This will vary from area to area according to the nature of the local problem. That is to say, there is no single universal solution. Such a plan will involve surveys of the number of visitors, their patterns of movement, and the specific causes of footpath damage. It will also attempt to determine the **ecological capacity** of the area (the maximum level of use that can occur before unacceptable changes take place in the flora, fauna and soil). It will also require the establishment of **control plots** to act as a **baseline**, so that the species composition of trampled and non-trampled areas can be

This is a tightly written paragraph containing a lot of information. The temptation is to elaborate on these points, but time forbids such a digression.

You have a free choice of 'problem'. Obviously, your choice will be determined by what you feel most confident to write about.

Notice how the results of two surveys are introduced into this paragraph. These provide the context for the more detailed discussion of footpath erosion which follows.

compared. Once this type of information has been assembled, a number of strategies should become more evident. These might include the following:

1. **Regrading of slopes**. Erosion is significantly greater on slopes exceeding 14° than on slopes below this critical threshold. Thus, footpaths might be re-routed to achieve lower gradients, or steps might be built into steep sections.

2. **Resurfacing**. The durability of surfaces might be improved in places by the use of duck-boards, sleepers, gravel dressing or even tarmac.

3. **Replanting**. This might involve the replacement of **vulnerable** plant species (easily destroyed by trampling) by **resilient** species (resistant to trampling). The aim is to establish plant communities which regenerate quickly. This might involve...

4. **Seeding, application of fertilisers and re-turfing**.

5. **Drainage improvements**. Diversion of surface water from paths might reduce erosion.

6. **Reduced usage of footpaths**. This might be achieved in various ways: for example by increasing car-parking charges at access points, developing alternate paths and trails, re-routing paths in areas of most severe erosion, by developing alternate attractions, by educating the public about the nature of the problem, etc.

7. **Closure of footpaths**. Prohibited access for a period of time might allow repairs to be carried out and vegetation to regenerate.

All of these strategies involve considerable cost. They also involve modifications to the natural environment. Controlled usage and limited access also undermine the basic principles of the early campaigners for National Parks. The achievement of a balanced package of remedies is the aim of a good management plan.

> Normally, numbered lists or catalogues of this type are not regarded as an appropriate style of presentation in essay answers. This list is just about acceptable, because, with its numbered sections, this is not a formal essay question. Alternatively, the seven points could have been merged into a single paragraph.

General Comments

This question brings together two important themes: firstly, the management and protection of rural environments; and, secondly, the impact of tourists and visitors on the countryside. Questions on countryside management can be quite varied, and are difficult to anticipate and 'spot'. They may relate to either natural habitats or agro-ecosystems. They may be concerned with the management of resources in rural areas, or the management of tourism, or the planning of small rural settlements and rural communities. In contrast, questions on the impact of tourists on the countryside are relatively predictable, and frequently focus on environmental and ecological damage in 'honeypot' locations.

Related questions

1   Make a critical evaluation of the impact, both positive and negative, of tourists on small rural settlements.

2   Describe how you would organise a survey into the problems of footpath erosion in a popular rural tourist destination.

3   How successful do you think the National Parks in Britain have been in fulfilling the expressed aims at the time of their establishment?

Question 18

(a) Comment briefly on the causes of soil erosion. (5 marks)

(b) What farming techniques serve to prevent or reduce soil erosion? (10 marks)

(c) What may be done, if anything, to restore the productivity and stability of areas already seriously damaged by soil erosion? (10 marks)

These are very predictable questions on a subject which is a great favourite with examiners. Given its frequent occurrence on A-level papers, 'soil erosion' is a topic which you should prepare carefully. It might be questioned in sections of the exam dealing with human impacts on the environment, or could appear on papers in physical geography which include a section on pedology.

There is only a limited number of obvious themes that can be questioned: causes of soil erosion, types of soil erosion, farming and forestry techniques which lead to soil erosion, and remedial practices aimed at restoring the productivity of areas damaged by soil erosion. Three of those four are included here. Make sure that you have good notes. Read the relevant sections in at least a couple of textbooks, identify some of the key contributors to the subject area, and learn a range of examples that you can introduce into your answer.

Answer

Guidance notes

(a) Causes of soil erosion

The term soil erosion has been defined quite simply as 'the wearing away and loss of top-soil, mainly by the action of wind and rain' (W.G. Moore, *Dictionary of Geography*, 1988).

In nature a delicate balance exists between the composition and texture of the soil in any area and the vegetation cover which it supports. That balance can be upset by human activity, such as the introduction of field crops or grazing animals, or the clearance of steep, forested hillsides. Natural vegetation

A definition can make an effective opening statement which can then be developed in subsequent paragraphs, as here.

The question doesn't ask specifically about different types of soil erosion. Some are mentioned in passing, but with little or no amplification. Avoid the temptation to describe the various types in detail.

Different climatic environments in which soil erosion is prevalent are identified. In the final paragraph of this section the occurrence of soil erosion in Britain is mentioned together with some important researchers on the problem.

This section of the answer is mainly about good farming practices. Notice how, in paragraphs one, two and three of this section, the discussion becomes progressively more specific.

protects the soil in a variety of ways, and helps to prevent and to check soil erosion.

Soil erosion results from **physical processes** such as rain wash or the blowing away of top-soil by strong winds. This general, widespread removal of soil by wind or rain, usually on gently sloping ground, is referred to as **sheet erosion**. The natural processes of wind and rain become destructive as a result of the **human mismanagement** of the land, leading to soil exhaustion and deterioration as a first stage in the process of soil erosion. In tropical areas, forest clearance and the burning of undergrowth frequently leave the land susceptible to rain wash and progressive damage by **rill and gully erosion**. More specific causes of soil erosion include the practice of mono-culture, inadequate crop rotations, lack of fertiliser, ploughing down steep slopes, etc.

Soil erosion can also be related to climatic conditions, such as the amount, intensity and seasonal distribution of rainfall. In areas with a marked wet and dry season, such as tropical savanna and monsoon areas, soils are particularly at risk. Heavy rain, falling on desiccated, cracked soils at the end of the dry season, is more likely to wash away top-soil than gentle rain in areas where precipitation is evenly distributed throughout the year. Similarly, strong prevailing winds are likely to cause most damage in areas of arid or semi-arid climate such as the 'Dust Bowl' states on the high plains of the USA.

Soil erosion has probably existed since early times. However, what is clear is that the extent and seriousness of soil erosion has greatly increased during the twentieth century. Extensive areas of soil loss are now found in North and South America, Asia, Africa, Australia, and on a lesser scale in parts of Europe too. The work of R. Evans, R.P.C. Morgan, J. Boardman and others has drawn attention to soil erosion as a growing problem in the UK, especially in areas of light sands, loams and peats.

(b) Prevention/reduction of soil erosion

The causes and effects of soil erosion have been extensively studied in many different types of natural environment. The processes involved are clearly understood, and there is a general consensus about what constitutes good and bad land management. Efficient husbandry, which encourages **soil conservation**, means working in harmony with nature, rather than seeking to exploit it for short-term gain or profit.

Good farming techniques strive to maintain the composition, texture, nutrient levels and fertility of the natural soil cover. This requires careful consideration of the **carrying capacity** of the land so that reasonable limits are not exceeded. This in turn involves the selection of appropriate crops, the use of sensible crop rotations, an avoidance of monoculture, the diversification of production, regular applications of humus, fertiliser and manure, and control of livestock numbers. Good farming systems also allow the soil to recover after cropping and grazing, and involve the replacement of essential soil nutrients.

Preventative measures also require the use of appropriate **farming techniques**. For example, in areas where there is a risk of rain wash or rill and gully development, contour ploughing is essential. Compacted tractor tracks running down-slope become channels for rain-water, and can easily develop into rills and gullies. Transverse hillside ditches can be cut to intersect runoff, and uncultivated strips of land can be left to achieve the same result. In areas where topsoil is at risk from wind erosion, the timing of sowing and harvesting should aim to ensure that fields are never left bare and unplanted during dry periods. It may even be necessary to apply a mulch cover in order to maintain soil moisture and combat wind erosion. Where deflation is a potential problem, shelter belts of trees should never be felled, and hedgerows should never be removed.

Reference to areas suffering from soil erosion can often provide an indication of what not to do; that is to say, they act as indicators of bad practice. For example, a recent study by D. Robinson and J. Blackman of soil erosion at various localities on the South Downs noted that the cropping pattern followed by many downland farmers leaves the ground with little or no vegetation cover during the autumn which is the wettest time of the year. They also noted that the recent amalgamation of fields has increased the area contributing to runoff on many slopes, and has removed checks on downslope movement of soil. They also refer to the use of increasingly powerful farm machinery and the cultivation of increasingly steep slopes. They note too that tractors are compelled to drive up and down slopes, leaving deep tracks aligned across the contours. During rainstorms, runoff is concentrated along these lines. Other adverse practices noted by Robinson and Blackman include the burning of stubble rather than ploughing it back into the soil, the absence of grass leys from rotations, the declining use of animal manure because livestock are no longer reared on many farms, and the pulverisation of the soil to an extremely fine tilth in order to obtain maximum efficiency from selective herbicides. The combination of these practices, they believe, lies at the heart of a growing problem of soil loss in many downland areas.

In a discussion about what constitutes good practice, it is also appropriate to mention the lessons that can be learnt from bad practice and to draw attention to techniques which should be avoided.

As in the previous section, the material here also becomes progressively more specific and detailed. In most descriptive passages in your answers, it is best to work from the general to the particular.

(c) Restoration of productivity and stability

Once soil erosion has taken place, the results are essentially permanent and largely irreversible. Soil that has been eroded from a particular locality has gone for ever. It is carried downstream where it contributes to fluvial or lacustrine silting or coastal progradation, or is carried by the wind far from its area of origin. However, where the original soil cover has only been partially removed, the process can be arrested and the area restored to productivity and stability by a series of remedial measures.

To a large extent remedial action is simply the correction of bad practice. For example, grazing should be severely reduced or terminated to allow grassland to regenerate. The nutrient status and texture of arable land can be improved by the careful rotation of 'climatically-suitable' crops. A plant cover should be maintained at critical times of the year when the risk of erosion is greatest. In areas of severe damage, land can be taken out of production altogether. Examples of this approach include the Soil Bank Program (1956) and Conservation Reserve Program (1985) in the USA whereby farmers were paid a 'rent' not to cultivate their land for three to ten years.

Measures can be taken to prevent further gully enlargement, such as the building of barriers and retaining walls to trap the downslope movement of soil. Covers of brushwood and planting with vines and trailing plants may help to bind together badly eroded surfaces. Contour ploughing, the cutting of transverse ditches and the retention of uncultivated strips of land can all help to stabilise the soil cover of sloping ground. The ultimate remedy might be the cutting of terraces on steep slopes. Where wind erosion has been active, shelter belts of trees can be planted and hedgerows replaced. The soil surface should not be reduced to a fine, powdery tilth, but should be left 'rough' and covered with some form of mulch to retain moisture and protect the surface from the wind.

Best results are likely to be achieved by the formulation of a conservation plan for a whole drainage basin rather than single holdings. Without a broad, integrated view, remedies for one farm usually involve transferring the problem to another. In basin management schemes, the high ground near the watershed may be re-afforested, and river flow controlled by regulatory dams. Funds may be made available for the whole basin, and technical advisory and educational services established for all farmers within the area. Probably the best known integrated scheme of this type is that of the Tennessee Valley Authority (TVA) which was set up in a region of severe erosion in the South-Eastern USA in 1933. The TVA Project has subsequently become a model of what can be achieved and has influenced

This is a classic example of drainage basin management which demonstrates large-scale integrated planning. It is described in many textbooks.

similar programmes elsewhere in the world. Ultimately, soil erosion is a result of over-exploitation, due to either greed, need or ignorance. Lasting progress can only be made when fundamental changes in attitudes towards the land have been achieved by education and example.

General Comments

Most examination boards include a section on pedology in the part of the syllabus dealing with physical geography. Typically, this will require the study of the processes of soil formation and the resultant variations in soil composition. You will also be expected to know something about the distribution and characteristics of zonal soils at global scale, as well as the characteristics of common British soil types. The subject of this question is soil erosion, which is almost always a result of human activity such as inappropriate farming techniques or deforestation. However, you are likely to feel more confident in writing the answer, and will probably produce a better answer if you have at least some basic knowledge of pedology.

Related questions

1   In Britain, many modern farming practices have had the effect of increasing soil erosion. Explain why this is the case.

2   To what extent are the causes of soil erosion different in tropical and mid-latitude regions?

3   Examine the problems of soil erosion in any *one* selected country or region.

Question 19

Describe and comment on the main demographic changes which have taken place in the United Kingdom since 1950.

Tackling the question

In one respect this is a straightforward and relatively easy question. It is largely descriptive. In essence it requires a well-organised, structured account of the main demographic changes which have taken place in the UK during the second half of the twentieth century, together with some commentary on the main features of those changes. On the other hand, to produce a good answer, you need a great deal of factual information about birth rates, death rates, etc. The obvious way in which you can make this task manageable is to divide your description into three main sections, each one dealing with a particular component of demographic change; namely, fertility, mortality and migration. That is the scheme followed here.

The sample answer contains a graph which is unrealistically detailed for an A-level answer. It would be an exceptional candidate that could produce such a graph under examination conditions. On the other hand, you should be able to produce a simplified version of this graph sufficient to show the main demographic trends in broad outline. As a revision exercise, you might consider how the diagram could be reduced in complexity and made more appropriate for an exam answer.

Answer

The components of population are identified in the introduction. They are then considered in turn in the main body of the essay.

Between 1951 and 1991, the total population of the UK increased from 50.4 million to 57.6 million. This growth of numbers was the product of three processes known collectively as the **components of demographic change** or the **basic demographic processes**. Changes in total numbers over a given period of time are determined by the number of births occurring (fertility), the number of deaths occurring (mortality) and the number of persons moving in and out of the area concerned (migration). Clearly, many different permutations of these three variables are possible. The number of births may exceed the number of deaths (natural increase) or vice versa (natural decrease). The difference between the number of immigrants and number of emigrants (net migration balance) may be positive or negative, and may augment or reduce or even cancel out any natural increase or decrease. The relationships between these three variables may be expressed by a formula for population change:

$$P_1 = P_0 + B - D \pm M$$

P_1 is the total population at the end of a given time period; P_0 is the total population at the beginning of the time period; B is the number of births occurring during the period in question; D is the number of deaths, and M is the net migration balance (positive or negative). Consideration of postwar demographic change in the UK obviously requires consideration of these key variables: namely, fertility, mortality and migration. They will be examined in turn.

Information about the three components of demographic change in the UK can be derived from various data sources. The Registrar General's Office is responsible for the continuous collection and publication of vital statistics relating to births, deaths, marriages, divorces, etc. These data can be found in the various Returns published by the Registrar General's Office. They can also be consulted in summary form in the *Annual Abstract of Statistics* published by HMSO. Essential material for the study of postwar demographic change is also provided by the *UK Census Reports* for 1951, 1961, 1971, 1981 and 1991 together with the report of the 10% sample census of 1966.

Identification of data sources is not specifically requested in the question. If you are running short of time this paragraph is expendable.

Fertility may be expressed in various ways. For example, reference can simply be made to the total number of live births per year. Alternatively, total births can be related to total population to give a crude birth rate, or to the number of women in the reproductive age group (15–44 years) to give a general fertility rate. In the UK the total number of births rose steadily from about 800,000 in 1950 to a peak of over 1 million (1,015,000) in 1964. This was the so-called 'baby boom' of the 1950s and early 1960s. In 1964 the crude birth rate of the UK stood at an all time high of 18.8 per thousand. In 1963 the oral contraceptive pill first became available to women, and in 1968 the Abortion Act legalised abortion in certain circumstances. The combination of these two factors, especially the former, initiated a down-turn in birth rate which continued for 13 years until 1977 when the number of live births was 657,000 to give a crude birth rate of 11.8 per thousand. For two years, 1976 and 1977, the number of births was actually less than the number of deaths, and the country briefly experienced a natural decrease of population. Subsequently, during the 1980s, the number of births rose to about 700,000 per year to give a crude birth rate of about 13 per thousand. This slight up-turn in birth rate has been explained as a result of couples postponing the start of a family. Between 1965 and 1985 the average age of mothers having their first child increased from 21 to 27 years of age.

This paragraph contains a great deal of statistical detail. A more generalised treatment would be acceptable, provided that you convey the main trends.

Mortality rates show little variation, making this a very easy component to describe.

Mortality in the UK since 1950 has been subject to far less fluctuation than fertility during the same period. The total number of deaths in the UK each year since 1950 has been between 600,000 and 700,000. Crude death rates during a period of 45 years have stubbornly remained within the range of 11 to 13 per thousand. This is significantly higher than the crude mortality rate of most other countries of north-west Europe. The **causes of death** have shown little change over the period with diseases of the circulatory system and cancer firmly established as the main killing diseases and jointly accounting for over 70% of all deaths by the 1980s. The failure of the UK to reduce its mortality rate during the second half of the twentieth century has been attributed to various factors; namely, declining standards of health care, the maintenance of a large stock of obsolete slum housing, high unemployment rates and high levels of poverty and deprivation. In the late-1980s, infant mortality rates, probably the most sensitive indicator of the quality of the social and physical environment for human life, actually rose in many parts of the country.

Of the three components of population change, **migration** is by far the smallest numerically. Unfortunately, detailed statistics for the numbers of migrants entering and leaving the UK only extend back as far as 1964. Comprehensive statistics for the numbers of immigrants and emigrants are not available for

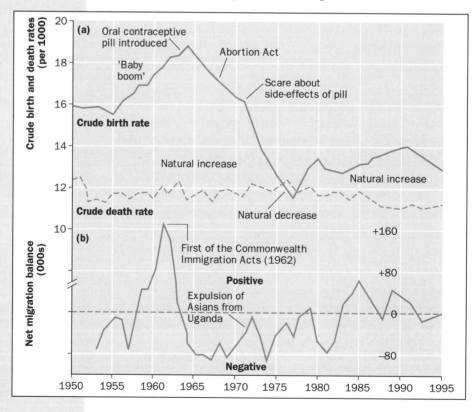

Figure 1 (a) Crude birth and death rates for the UK, 1950–1995
(b) Net migration balance, 1953–1995

the period of the 1950s and early-1960s when large numbers of West Indians and Asians entered the UK. Post-1964 statistics reveal considerable short-term fluctuations in the numbers of both immigrants and emigrants. However, with the exception of just two or three periods the net migration balance is a negative one; that is to say, in most years more people left than entered the UK. Despite the popular myths about the flood of immigrants entering the UK, the reality is that the UK is a net 'exporter' of population in most years. Since the early 1960s, the numbers entering the UK have been checked and reduced by a succession of Immigration Acts (1962, 1968, 1972, etc.) designed to make the conditions of entry more demanding and settlement in the UK more difficult. The short-term fluctuations of both immigration and emigration appear to be related to 'push' factors in the source areas as well as 'pull' factors in the destination area. Thus, peaks of immigration appear to be related to particular overseas events. For example, the expulsion of Asians from Uganda by President Amin in 1972 corresponds with a minor peak in the flow of immigrants into the UK.

One of the most obvious demographic changes in postwar Britain has been its transformation into a **multiracial and multicultural society**. Prior to 1991, the UK census did not include questions on race and ethnicity, so that it was impossible to obtain precise information about the size and distribution of minority groups. However, 'place-of-birth' statistics derived from the census show that by 1981 about 6% of the UK population was 'overseas-born'. (No information was collected about the number of children born in the UK but having overseas-born parents.) The total percentage of overseas-born population is not large, but is very unevenly distributed. Racial and ethnic minorities tend to cluster in the inner city districts of particular towns and cities.

International migration affects the total numbers and demographic structure (age structure, ethnic structure, sex ratio, etc.) of any country, while **internal migration** within a country simply changes the overall distribution and demographic structure of particular regions, but has no effect on total numbers. A rather specialised form of internal migration is **retirement migration** which has produced concentrations of elderly people in many coastal towns in East Anglia, Southern England, the South-West peninsula and North and Mid-Wales. During the early postwar years, the broad pattern of internal movement in the UK tended to be away from Scotland, Northern Ireland, Northern England and Wales towards the more affluent regions of Eastern, Southern and South-East England. However, there is evidence to suggest that this trend has slowed down and may even have reversed itself. The period 1950–90 was one of counter-urbanisation with the largest cities showing a consis-

The migration process is described in this paragraph. The following two paragraphs examine the effects of both international and internal migration on population distribution and composition.

tent loss of numbers as population moved away from the overcrowded, congested inner city areas to less expensive, and more salubrious areas in the outer suburbs and beyond. Thus, in 1981, London's population fell below 7 million for the first time since 1901, and heavy losses of population were recorded in Glasgow, Manchester, Birmingham, Liverpool and Newcastle.

In summary, the main determinant of demographic change in the UK since 1950 has been birth rate. This has shown the greatest fluctuation during the period in question. In contrast, mortality rate has remained stable throughout. Net migration balance has been negative in most years, but has been insignificant numerically compared with the other two variables. Fertility and mortality have produced changes in total numbers and changes in age structure. International migration has affected total numbers, but only to a very limited degree; its main effect has been to modify the demographic composition of the population. The main effect of internal migration has been to modify the spatial distribution of population.

In an essay such as this, which conveys a large amount of factual information, the best type of conclusion is probably a summary. That is what is attempted here.

General comments

Inevitably the section of your syllabus dealing with population geography will require that you study the three components of population change — fertility, mortality and migration. You will be expected to understand how various combinations of these factors produce population growth or decline as well as determining the composition of any population. The basic demographic processes should not be studied in isolation. They should be related to one particular country. The United Kingdom, the subject of this question, is the obvious example.

Related questions

1 Write an explanatory account of the spatial variations in mortality rates in the United Kingdom.

2 In what ways has the population composition of the United Kingdom changed during the second half of the twentieth century?

3 Describe and explain the spatial distribution of any one ethnic minority group in any one British city.

Question 20

Describe and comment on the use of the Lorenz Curve
in the analysis of population distribution patterns.

This question is about the use of a technique which is widely employed in the analysis of distribution patterns. The Lorenz Curve can be used to analyse many different types of spatial pattern, but the question here relates it specifically to population distribution. Firstly, you are asked to describe the use of the technique; that is to say, the methodology of its application. Secondly, you are required to comment on its use. In that context, you should draw attention to any limitations, as well as attempting to evaluate its strengths and weaknesses as a technique of analysis.

You may find that the style and language of the answer present problems. The technique itself is easy to use, but difficult to describe. What is simple in practice, is awkward to relate. The first part of the answer virtually requires the language of an instruction manual. In the sample answer, a hypothetical example is used to facilitate description of the method, but even that is not wholly satisfactory.

Answer

Guidance notes

In certain types of geographical study, it may be appropriate to simply describe patterns of population distribution in broad, subjective, impressionistic terms. On the basis of a visual appraisal of distribution maps, population in a particular area might be described as concentrated, scattered, evenly spaced, and so on. However, for other types of analysis a more precise, objective, quantitative form of description might be necessary. For this reason, a variety of statistical techniques have been devised by geographers for measuring and expressing population density, centrality, dispersion, concentration and spacing. The Lorenz Curve is one such technique. It is a **graphical device**, widely used to express the unevenness or concentration of population. It may be used for describing population in one specific area at a given point in time, or for studying changes in population distribution in a given area through time, or for comparing population spacing in one area with that in another.

Question 20

It is important to identify the type of data needed for the use of the technique.

At this point an example is introduced to facilitate description of the methodology.

The problem here is style and language. The description of how to use the technique is presented as a series of steps in order to make it as clear as possible.

This paragraph is concerned with interpretation of results; that is to say, the different forms that the Lorenz Curve can assume.

The Lorenz Curve can be used for areas which are sub-divided into smaller units for which data are available for size (area) and total population; for example, wards within a city area, parishes within a county, or states within a nation. The Lorenz Curve employs a square graph with the x- and y-axes having comparable scales, such as percentage units. Appropriate data are collected for sub-divisions of the total area being considered, and plotted on the graph. In the context of the analysis of population distribution, cumulative percentages of population are plotted on the x-axis and cumulative percentages of area on the y-axis. The method of construction is described below, using as an example the 1990 distribution of population in the USA.

Step 1 Rank the 49 contiguous states of the USA in descending order of **population density**. (District of Columbia, New Jersey, Rhode Island, Massachusetts, etc. down to Wyoming at Rank Number 49.)

Step 2 Decide on the number of plotting points to be used on the graph. In this example, it might be appropriate to use 12 plotting points. In this way the individual states could be dealt with in 11 groups of four plus one group of five.

Step 3 Take the first group of four states; namely, the four states with the highest population densities (District of Columbia, New Jersey, Rhode Island and Massachusetts). Sum their populations and express the result as a percentage of the total US population (7.0%). Sum their areas and express the result as a percentage of the total US area (0.5%). Thus, it is shown that 7.0% of the US population occupies 0.5% of the US area. The co-ordinate for these two values is the first plotting point on the graph.

Step 4 Repeat this process for the top eight states in the density ranking. This gives the second plotting point. Similarly, calculate values for the 12th, 16th and subsequent multiples of four. Plotting of the 12 resultant co-ordinates will give the result shown in Figure 1.

The Lorenz Curve will always lie between the diagonal and the x-axis of the graph. These represent the two extreme and totally hypothetical positions for the curve. The diagonal would be produced by a **perfectly even distribution** of population. The x-axis would be produced by **total concentration** of population (100% of the population occupying 0% of the area). Actual

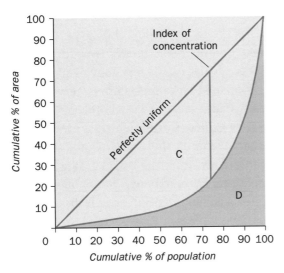

Figure 1 Lorenz Curve for the distribution of
US population, 1980

curves lie between these extremes. The main problem is that of interpreting particular curves. Clearly, a shallow curve which lies close to the diagonal signifies a population distribution with a strong tendency towards even spacing. A deep concave curve signifies a much greater degree of concentration (see Figure 2).

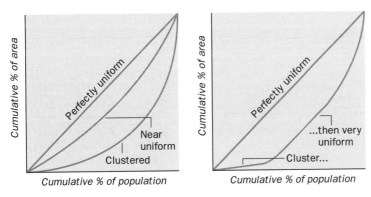

Figure 2 Variations in the form of the Lorenz Curve

In some cases, a more precise analysis of the Lorenz Curve is required. This involves calculating the area below the curve and expressing it as a percentage of the area below the diagonal. A value of 90%, for example, would represent almost perfectly uniform distribution of population, whereas a value of 20–30% would indicate considerable population clustering. The so-called **Gini Co-efficient** (G) or **Gini's Concentration Ratio** is rather similar. This expresses the area between the diagonal and the Lorenz Curve (C) as a fraction of the total area beneath the diagonal (C + D) (see Figure 1):

$$\frac{C}{C + D}$$

It is likely, if you have used the technique, that you will have simply made a visual interpretation of the resulting curves. The use of the Gini Co-efficient is something of an optional extra. Only the best answers are likely to mention its use. On the other hand, the Index of Concentration is very easy to use. That should be mentioned.

The concluding paragraph attempts a balanced appraisal of the technique, mentioning both strengths and limitations.

The problem with both of these measures is that of calculating the areas above and below the curve. One method is to superimpose a grid of small squares over the graph, and then to estimate the number of squares above and below the curve. However, this method lacks precision, is very time-consuming, and is not particularly satisfactory. Another approach is to calculate the **Index of Concentration** which is simply the maximum vertical distance between the Lorenz Curve and the diagonal. This may be obtained from the original data as the maximum difference between the cumulative percentages of the two sets of values (area and population) or may be simply measured directly from the graph (see Figure 1).

The Lorenz Curve provides a useful means of describing and comparing population distribution patterns. It allows either a simple visual evaluation to be made of particular patterns, or, by calculating the Gini Co-efficient, it enables precise, quantitative descriptions and comparisons to be made. It is particularly useful in allowing comparisons to be made of distribution patterns in areas which differ greatly in size. Its main disadvantage is that it is time-consuming to construct. The Lorenz Curve cannot reveal variations in population concentration and dispersion within areal units. It follows, therefore, that it gives best results when used on areas which are sub-divided into large numbers of small units. Despite its limitations, it has long been a widely-used technique of population analysis.

General Comments

This is one of several questions in the book which require comment on the application and limitations of a well-known technique of geographical analysis. (Questions 1, 30 and 34 are similar in type.) One of the aims of the A-level examination is to test your understanding of various practical skills and techniques of data analysis and interpretation. Asking you to write an essay about a particular technique is one way of doing that. A better way is by means of a data-response question. Be prepared for a question on the Lorenz Curve and similar techniques in that section of your exam.

Related questions

1 Describe and comment on the use of the nearest-neighbour statistic in the analysis of rural settlement patterns.

2 Discuss the relative advantages and disadvantages of each of the following types of statistical map: (a) isopleth map; (b) choropleth map; (c) quantitative dot map.

3 (a) Describe the data required and the method employed to construct a population pyramid.

(b) Describe different types of age-index of population and the manner of their calculation.

(c) Comment on the relative usefulness of population pyramids and age-indices in the study of the age composition of populations.

Question 21

Describe and evaluate the various models and theories which have been developed to explain patterns and processes of migration.

Tackling the question

This particular question is somewhat different from those normally set on the subject of migration. It requires a review and evaluation of the various models and theories which have been developed to aid our understanding of the patterns and processes of migration. In other words, the focus is clearly on the theoretical aspects of migration rather than empirical case studies. The sample answer uses a chronological approach. It starts with the late nineteenth-century ideas of Ravenstein, through the mid twentieth-century mathematical models of Zipf and Stouffer, and concludes with the postwar behavioural approach of Bogue and others. In questions dealing with the development of ideas and theory, a chronological approach usually provides a perfectly adequate essay plan. Your plan is ready-made; one paragraph per contributor arranged in chronological sequence.

Answer

The opening paragraph 'sets the scene' by simply defining migration, identifying two types, and mentioning the limitations of the database.

Migration, one of the three components of population change, is defined in the *UN Demographic Yearbooks* as 'a movement of population involving a change of permanent residence of substantial duration'. A distinction is normally made between international migration which involves the crossing of an international boundary, and internal migration which refers to population movements within a national territory. One of the basic problems in the study of migration is the poor quality of the data available. International migration statistics are rarely comparable from one country to another due to differing definitions and methods of data collection, and very few countries publish detailed statistical accounts of population movements within their borders. It is somewhat surprising, therefore, in view of the paucity of the database, that there is in fact a long history of attempts to formulate laws and theories to explain patterns and processes of migration. Such work has derived not only from geography, but also from sociology, economics and mathematics.

One of the earliest workers in this field was **E.G. Ravenstein** who, in two papers presented to the Royal Statistical Society in 1885 and 1889, proposed his so-called Laws of Migration. Ravenstein examined many aspects of the migration process, including the relative importance of rural–urban and inter-urban migration, the relative mobility of males and females, and the effects of technological developments (transport and communications) on the volume of migration. However, his most important contribution was in drawing attention to the principle of chain or **stage migration**. According to Ravenstein, 'Migration occurs in a series of stages. The inhabitants of the country immediately surrounding a town of rapid growth flock into it; the gaps thus left by the rural population are filled by migrants from more remote districts, until the attractive force of a rapidly growing city makes its influence felt, step by step, in the most remote corner of the kingdom. Migrants enumerated in a certain centre of absorption consequently grow less with distance but are also proportionate to the size of the native population which furnishes them.' In this statement, Ravenstein is alluding to both the 'friction of distance' on the volume of migration and also to the influence of the size of source and destination centres on the volume of migration between them. Although his theory lacks the rigour and objectivity of most modern research, it is not unreasonable to regard Ravenstein as the 'father' of migration theory.

Subsequent studies have tended to support and substantiate Ravenstein's broad generalisations about the nature of the migration process. Much later, many of the concepts embodied in his Laws of Migration came to be re-examined and re-stated in more precise mathematical terms. For example, his observations on the 'friction of distance' were expressed with more precision in 1940 by G.K. Zipf, in the form of the Inverse Distance Law. According to Zipf, 'Volume of migration is inversely proportional to the distance travelled by migrants'. This may be expressed mathematically as follows:

$$N_{ij} \propto \frac{1}{D_{ij}}$$

N_{ij} is the number of migrants moving between towns 'i' and 'j', and D_{ij} is the distance separating the two towns. This simply gives precision to the notion that many migrants travel short distances and relatively few move over long distances.

At about the same time, **S.A. Stouffer** examined the effects of two variables on migration flows; namely, distance and opportunity defined in terms of available housing. Others, applying Stouffer's ideas, have defined opportunity in terms of employment opportunities. These two factors are brought together in Stouffer's **Theory of Intervening Opportunity**,

The chronological review starts with Ravenstein. For many years he was a neglected figure, but increasingly is seen as the founder of modern migration theory. You should be familiar with his Laws of Migration for the examination.

This paragraph demonstrates the link between Ravenstein's early work and the more modern approach typified by the gravity model.

Notice how each of the subsequent laws/theories/models is presented both as a statement and also as a mathematical equation. Make sure that you understand the mathematical form of expression, and can present this material in both ways.

published in 1940. This states that 'the number of persons migrating over a given distance is directly proportional to the number of opportunities at that distance, and inversely proportional to the number of intervening opportunities'. Again, this may be expressed mathematically:

$$Nij \propto \frac{Oj}{Oij}$$

Nij is the number of migrants between 'i' and 'j', Oj is the number of opportunities at the destination 'j', and Oij is the number of intervening opportunities between the source and destination towns or districts.

Another interesting development has been the application of **gravity models** to migration study. Ravenstein's first law of migration implies that distance is a barrier to movement and that long-distance moves require exceptionally strong attractive forces. It may be argued, therefore, that the size of a destination centre will determine the strength of its attraction. At the same time, the volume of migration decreases with distance from source, so that a nearby small town may exercise the same attraction as a distant large city. These relationships may be expressed by means of the following formula:

$$Nij \propto \frac{Pi \times Pj}{Dij^a}$$

Nij is the number of migrants moving from town 'i' to town 'j'; Pi is the population of town 'i', and Pj is the population of town 'j'; Dij is the distance between the two towns, and 'a' is an exponent of distance, usually the square of distance, although other values can be substituted. According to the formula, the volume of migration between two towns is directly proportional to the product of their population sizes and inversely proportional to an exponent of the distance between them.

The gravity model contains many assumptions which cannot be fully justified. For example, it implies that the attraction of any destination town is simply a product of its population size; also that potential migrants have equal ease of movement in all directions. The migrant is reduced to the status of a robot making automatic and completely logical decisions based on the information included in the model. The gravity model fails to take into account the unpredictable, illogical and often inexplicable nature of much human decision-making. Not surprisingly, there followed a reaction to the abstract, mathematical approach typified by the gravity model.

This reaction took the form of the so-called **behavioural approach** to migration study. According to this point of view, any migration stream is the product of innumerable personal decisions by individuals and families about when to move,

This paragraph evaluates the gravity model and similar approaches. The final sentence in the paragraph provides a clear link with the final type of theoretical approach. Try to make these links between paragraphs where possible.

choice of destination and so forth. Thus, it is argued that, in order to understand any migration stream, one must consider the factors which influence those decisions. They may include, for example, the migrant's perception and evaluation of alternative destinations. The behavioural approach, typified by the work of **D.J. Bogue** and others, is concerned with the **psychology of decision-making** and questions of **environmental perception**. The main problem is that such matters are difficult to understand and to quantify.

At the present time, migration theory has become polarised into two basic approaches: the abstract, mathematical approach typified by the use of the gravity model; and a pseudo-psychological approach typified by various behavioural models. Neither is wholly satisfactory. The next development may be a model which combines the best features of the two approaches.

> The final paragraph is short and speculative, but serves to summarise the present position. Essays must have a conclusion, but keep it brief and to the point.

General comments

If your A-level syllabus includes a section on population geography (most do), then there is a good chance that you will be confronted with a question on some aspect of migration. It is, after all, one of just three components of population change. The topic is a relatively straightforward one, and should present few problems. Questions are usually concerned with the causes of migration (push–pull factors), or the processes of migration (volume and direction of flows), or the economic, demographic and social effects on both source and destination areas. In your revision of this topic it is a good idea to learn some case studies of actual, well-documented migration flows, both internal and international. Remember too that the gravity model could easily be tested with a data-response question.

Related questions

1 'Geographers are generally well informed about the origins, destinations and frequencies of migration but, in contrast, have only a very imprecise knowledge of the reasons for moving.' Discuss.

2 What kinds of problems can migration cause and solve?

3 'Migration patterns within Britain are increasingly influenced by the growing importance of lifestyle, quality of life and the self-fulfilment of individuals.' Discuss.

Question 22

Make a critical evaluation of the demographic transition model.

The concept of a transition from high birth rate/high death rate to low birth rate/low death rate is one of the central tenets of demography and forms a core theme within the subject. The demographic transition also forms a conceptual framework to which many other aspects of population change can be related; for example, population growth rates, causes of death (the epidemiological transition), expectation of life, proportion of children, proportion of elderly population, etc. The demographic transition model provides a context and helps us to understand the temporal variations of a wide range of demographic factors. Because of its importance, questions on the demographic model frequently appear on the A-level paper.

In this case, a critical evaluation of the model is required. Clearly, that involves more than mere description of the model, although it would seem reasonable to describe the model before attempting an evaluation. Demonstrate that you know what you are talking about before making judgements. So, describe the model first. Then, focus on both the usefulness of the model and also its limitations. To what extent can a model derived from the European experience have universal applicability? That is the big question. Attempt a synthesis of the opposing positions in the final paragraph.

Answer

In this opening paragraph the demographic transition model is simply defined. Names are given of some of the key contributors to the concept. These are not essential, but might be expected in the best answers.

The demographic transition model is a model of population evolution. It is a **stage-model** which purports to demonstrate and predict a series of stages through which any nation will pass as its population evolves from the high fertility and high mortality of traditional society to the low fertility and low mortality of modern society. The demographic transition model has its origins in work by W.S. Thompson (1929), K. Davis (1945) and F.W. Notestein (1945), but their early statements about changes in fertility and mortality through time have been refined, modified and extended by subsequent writers.

The demographic transition model is based on the experience of population evolution in Western Europe and North America since the mid-eighteenth century. The reason for this Western emphasis is clear. It is only in Europe and North America that an unbroken sequence of census returns extends sufficiently far back in time to provide the empirical data base on which theorising about demographic evolution could be based. In Scandinavia, census records extend back to the mid-eighteenth century; in the USA, the first census was held in 1790; Britain and France followed in 1801. In contrast, the first modern census was not held in China until 1953 when more than one-fifth of the world's population was enumerated for the first time. Understandably, therefore, the demographic transition model was based on the Western, rather than the non-Western, experience. The extent to which the theory is culturally transferable will be considered later.

This paragraph follows logically from the introduction. It elaborates on the development of the model, and establishes the fact that it is based on the Western experience and why that should be so.

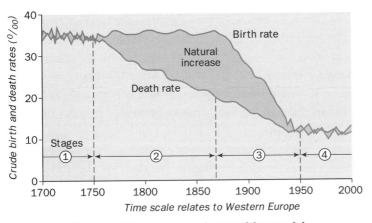

Figure 1 The demographic transition model

This diagram is so important that you should be able to reproduce it under examination conditions. It is one of a relatively small number of diagrams that you should commit to memory. In fact, if you really understand it, then it is not difficult to reconstruct it from memory.

In its most common form of presentation, the demographic transition model is shown as having four stages or regimes (see Figure 1). In **Stage 1**, the so-called primitive demographic regime, fertility and mortality both stand at very high levels, between $30^0/_{00}$ and $40^0/_{00}$. Under these circumstances, population growth is slow and intermittent, since a large number of births is cancelled out by a similarly large number of deaths. This situation prevailed in Britain until the mid-eighteenth century. At present, it is seen in just a very small number of Central African nations.

Stage 2 is referred to as the early expanding or youthful demographic regime. This stage is characterised by a decline in mortality rate while fertility continues to remain high. The result is a very rapid natural increase of population, accompanied by an ageing of the population. These conditions persisted in Britain until about 1870. Present fertility and mortality statistics suggest that most developing nations are currently in this type of situation.

This and the following sections describe the various stages of the model. As a general rule, numbered lists or catalogues of points should be avoided in essays. Essays should be in continuous prose and not look like a set of notes. However, this is a relatively short list — just four stages — and is acceptable.

Stage 3, the late-expanding demographic regime, sees the mortality rate continuing to fall, but fertility also starts to decline. The rate of natural increase is less than in Stage 2 but, by this time, there is a very large base population, so that the application of even a modest rate of natural increase produces a very large increase in actual numbers. Stages 2 and 3 are characterised by very rapid population growth.

Finally, in **Stage 4**, the mature or low-fluctuating demographic regime, both mortality and fertility rates become stabilised at relatively low levels, usually 10 per thousand or even less. Natural increase is therefore low; in a few instances, deaths may even exceed births, so that a natural decrease of population occurs. A handful of West European nations, together with Japan, may be said to have reached this final stage in the demographic transition.

The basic questions which have to be asked about the demographic transition model concern its value as a predictive model. Can it be assumed that, because the nations of Western Europe passed through a series of clearly defined stages of population change, other nations will follow the same evolutionary sequence? Will the demographic transition necessarily occur at some future time in the developing nations as it did in Europe in the past? Is the same sequence of stages inevitable? Will the developing nations require the same length of time to pass through Stages 2 and 3 as did the European nations? Most demographers would probably answer 'no' to all of these questions. Increasingly, the demographic transition model is seen as an interpretation of European population history rather than a predictive theory with universal application.

It has frequently been noted that present-day conditions in developing nations are very different from those of the late-eighteenth and nineteenth centuries when Europe experienced its most rapid population growth. Most developing nations enter Stage 2 with far larger populations than those of eighteenth-century Europe at the same stage of evolution. Furthermore, the eighteenth- and nineteenth-century rates of population increase in Europe were far lower than those of present-day developing nations. In Europe, the period of most rapid population growth went hand in hand with a rising tide of prosperity; that is certainly not the case in developing countries at the present time. In addition, massive emigration to the New World did much to relieve population pressure in Europe during the late-nineteenth and early-twentieth centuries. That sort of outlet is certainly not available to the present developing nations.

It has also been suggested that the length of time required to make the transition from high to low mortality and fertility might vary widely from nation to nation. In Europe, the transition took about 200 years. The developing nations might be able

At this point the focus of the essay shifts from description to evaluation. The question of universality is raised in this paragraph.

Differences between the European nations when they were in Stage 2 and the developing nations which are currently in Stage 2 are emphasised here.

The question of the time-scale of the model is raised here. Will the developing nations be able to achieve low fertility and low to achieve the same transition in a far shorter time as a result of economic aid, technical assistance, birth control programmes, improved education, etc. Indeed, it is essential that they do so, for a world increase of population of almost 75 million per year cannot be sustained for much longer without catastrophic consequences.

The demographic transition model is limited in its application. It has been said that 'the theory lacks rigour; it has logical inconsistencies; it involves a hotchpotch of causal variables and cannot be expected to have universal applicability'. (R. Woods) On the other hand, if it is accepted that it is place-specific, then it can provide a useful measure against which other patterns of population evolution may be compared and evaluated.

mortality in a much shorter time than the European nations?

In the concluding paragraph an attempt is made to produce a balanced evaluation, mentioning both the useful aspects as well as the limitations of the model.

General Comments

Population geography is not simply concerned with spatial variations in the components of population change. The study also has a temporal aspect. It is important to appreciate global trends in population change, and especially to be able to make detailed contrasts between the demographic evolution of developed and developing nations. From the examiner's point of view, a question on the demographic transition model is an ideal way of testing a variety of concepts in a single question. That is another reason why it is such a popular topic.

Related questions

1 Examine the social and economic implications of the simultaneous long-term reduction of birth rate and death rate in any country.

2 In what ways might the demographic evolution of the developing nations differ from that experienced by the nations of Europe?

3 Describe and explain why the age composition of countries differs according to the stage reached in the demographic transition.

Discuss the reasons for the continued occurrence of regional famine disasters in Africa.

Tackling the question

The occurrence of hunger and famine is frequently interpreted as the result of a disequilibrium between population and resources. This is the classical Malthusian view that, when population numbers outstrip the means of subsistence, an inevitable result will be a series of checks in the form of widespread famine, war and disaster. In Africa the occurrence of regional famine disasters is so frequent and persistent that a simple Malthusian explanation seems inadequate. This question is designed to seek out those other factors, special to Africa, which provide an explanation for this succession of disasters.

In planning an answer to this question, an important issue is whether or not to include a section on possible solutions to Africa's food problems — or is that irrelevant to this particular question? In this case, the causes and solutions are so interlinked that some reference to strategies for change is justified.

Answer

This is an unconventional way to open an essay. The passage quoted is also now quite dated. On the other hand, pictures and accounts of the Ethiopian famine disaster of the mid-1980s produced an unprecedented response worldwide, and focused attention, albeit briefly, on the enormous scale of the suffering and death in that part of Africa. A more recent account from Somalia, for example, could serve the same function in the essay.

In this paragraph the answer moves from the specific to the general; from conditions in Ethiopia in the mid-1980s to Africa as a whole.

'Dawn, and as the sun breaks through the piercing chill of the night on the plains outside Korem, it lights up a biblical famine, now, in the twentieth century. This place, say workers here, is the closest thing to hell on earth. Thousands of wasted people are coming here for help. Many find only death. They flood in every day from villages hundreds of miles away, felled by hunger, driven beyond the point of desperation. Death is all around.' (Michael Buerk's introduction to the first TV coverage of the Ethiopian famine disaster, BBC News, 23 October, 1984.)

For most people, Michael Buerk's moving description and the late Mohamed Amin's harrowing film provided their first awareness of the Ethiopian famine disaster of 1984/85. One result was a worldwide, voluntary fund-raising campaign on an unprecedented scale. However, what many people failed to realise was that hunger and malnutrition are constantly present in many parts of Africa, and that most of the resultant human suffering is continuous, unnoticed and unrecorded. It has been estimated, for example, that even in a 'normal' year as many as

100 million Africans are malnourished and severely hungry. Thus, the 1984/85 Ethiopian famine was just one of a long **succession of famine disasters** which struck Africa in the 1970s and 1980s. The names hit the headlines with depressing regularity and were then forgotten ... Mali, Niger, Chad, Sudan, Uganda, Somalia, Ethiopia, Angola, Botswana, Zimbabwe, Zambia and Mozambique.

Given this succession of disasters, the question must be asked, why do regional famines occur so frequently in Africa? In fact the causes are varied and complex, and there is no single, simple explanation. Most famines in Africa stem from a combination of factors. I.L. Griffiths and J.A. Binns have suggested five broad categories of explanation, and these will be used as a framework for discussing the question.

First, Griffiths and Binns refer to what they term the **natural disaster thesis**. This is the view that famines are caused by natural disasters such as droughts, floods, hurricanes, earthquakes, plagues of locusts, and so on. Closer examination suggests that this thesis is untenable. Typically, a natural disaster acts as the final 'trigger' in a situation in which the food situation is already precarious, but is not the prime cause. For example, to regard the Ethiopian famine simply as a result of drought or progressive desertification would be to misunderstand its true cause. Like most famine disasters, this was more a man-made catastrophe rather than a result of natural causes.

Secondly, there is the **Neo-Malthusian thesis**. Most African nations have very high rates of population growth (more than 3% per annum in some cases), while at the same time food production in many countries is actually declining. Statistics from the UN Food and Agriculture Organisation (FAO) show that food production in Africa declined by 1.2% per annum between 1975 and 1985. According to the Malthusian principle, this combination of rapid population growth and stagnant resource development must inevitably produce famine, starvation and misery. However, in order to advance this analysis, one must also consider why it has proved to be so difficult to increase food production in many parts of the continent. Part of the answer to that question is to be found in Griffiths and Binns' third category of explanation; namely, the underdevelopment thesis.

According to the **underdevelopment thesis**, many of Africa's contemporary problems have their roots in the colonial history of the continent. Colonialism, it is argued, was an exploitive economic system using cheap African labour to develop Africa's resources for the benefit of the capitalist nations of Europe. It placed emphasis on cash crops, neglected native food crops, encouraged farmers to migrate to plantations and mines as paid labourers, and generally neglected rural areas in favour of colonial towns and administrative centres. For these

The analysis of Africa's food problems by Griffiths and Binns is so highly structured that it provides a ready-made framework for the essay. This is quite acceptable, but the source of the plan should be made clear and acknowledged.

Notice how each category of explanation is allocated one paragraph in the answer. In each paragraph the causal explanation is identified and discussed in general terms, and then illustrated by reference to a particular area or example.

reasons, nations which prior to European intervention in Africa had been self-sufficient in food, now continue to pay a catastrophic price for their former exploitation by colonial powers. It is both ironic and symptomatic, for example, that throughout the Ethiopian famine, the country remained a net exporter of foodstuffs — mainly early vegetables for winter consumption in Europe.

Fourthly, there is the **interventionist thesis**. In this context it has been suggested by many writers that African nations suffer from excessive government intervention in their economic affairs. One effect, it is argued, is to keep food prices low for urban consumers at the expense of rural producers. Various government marketing boards and distribution agencies and other bureaucratic institutions, notorious for their inefficiency and corruption, have actually resulted in a decline in the production of staple foodstuffs in many nations. Even in times of famine, they have proved to be almost totally ineffective in the simple task of distributing food aid and medical supplies. In Ethiopia, thousands died while supplies of grain deteriorated and lay unused in coastal warehouses.

Finally, Griffiths and Binns refer to the **political immaturity thesis**. They note that many African nations inherited their national boundaries from former colonial powers, and that these boundaries frequently divide cultural, ethnic and tribal groups between neighbouring states, or bring together opposing factions within a single state. This has resulted in wars between nations and civil wars within nations. Military conflicts have involved the disruption of normal farming routines, the plundering of crops and livestock, the destruction of villages and scorched earth tactics, evacuation of populations, expulsion of relief agencies, destruction and closure of roads, and the division of funds and resources to the military. African nations involved in civil wars and internal conflicts in recent years include Sudan, Chad, Ethiopia, Uganda, Angola, Mozambique, Somalia, Rwanda and Zaire. Others have been engaged in international conflicts. The correlation between war-torn regions and famine regions in Africa is a close one.

Discussion of the causes of regional famine in Africa inevitably involves the question of **possible solutions** and the **long-term prospects** for these disaster areas. In the context, it is normal to distinguish between **short-term responses** (immediate food aid and medical supplies) and **long-term responses** (the eradication of the deep-seated causes of famine). Because the causes of famine are both complex and varied, it follows that there can be no single solution.

Long-term improvements in the food supply of famine-prone nations in Africa will require a combination of political and economic strategies. Change can only come about if

The final section of the essay moves on to possible solutions to the economic exploitation of Africa by the developed nations is terminated. This will require massive improvements in the terms of trade for African nations so that they derive greater income and benefit from their labours than at present. There should be a termination of civil and international wars, and a diversion of precious resources from military expenditure to economic development. The Organisation of African Unity (OAU) could play an important role in helping to bring that change about.

As well as political initiatives, economic changes will be required. There should be a reduction in cash crop production and greater encouragement for the cultivation of subsistence food crops. Increased trade and co-operation between African nations might be beneficial in any move away from cash crop production. Agricultural productivity could be raised from its present low level by long-term restoration of the ecological balance in environmentally degraded areas. This might involve programmes of reforestation, afforestation and soil conservation. Systems of water control and water storage could be initiated by the building of dams, reservoirs, irrigation canals and other hydraulic works. There should be improvements in the economic infrastructure of famine-prone nations, so that seeds and grain and other foodstuffs can be stored and distributed readily in times of need.

Improvements in rural living conditions are also necessary. Better housing, water supply, sanitation, health care and education would produce people better able to take initiatives, plan for their future and deal with crises more effectively. Simultaneously with all of these changes, the greatest efforts should be made to control and reduce present rates of population growth by the introduction of birth control policies. Of course, the costs of such programmes would be enormous, and far beyond the means of impoverished nations already burdened with debt. Improvements can only come about by **international effort and co-operation**. But, unless that effort is made, the certain future for many African nations is the misery of continuing famine disasters.

Africa's food crisis. This is not an irrelevant addition to the essay, even though a discussion of policy is not specifically requested in the question. A look towards the future is often an appropriate way to conclude an essay.

General comments

In essence this is a question about population and resources — in this case, food resources. This topic involves the concepts of overpopulation, underpopulation and optimum population. Make sure that you can define and discuss those. Questions on population and resources are sometimes at global scale, sometimes at continental scale (as here), and occasionally at national scale. They usually appear in the section of the exam on population geography, but some exams also include a section on global and regional disparities where they can also appear.

Related questions

1 To what extent do the ideas of Malthus provide an adequate explanation of the food shortages experienced in many developing nations?

2 Examine the problems involved in defining the term 'overpopulation'.

3 Evaluate the contribution of *two* of the following to our understanding of the relationships between population and resources: (a) Thomas Malthus; (b) Karl Marx; (c) Paul Ehrlich.

Critically examine von Thünen's Theory of Agricultural Land Use, assessing its relevance today.

Tackling the question

This is a very popular topic with examiners. Not only do questions on von Thünen's theory turn up with great frequency, they are also relatively predictable in their requirements. They almost always ask for discussion of the contemporary relevance of von Thünen's ideas. Does the theory have any relevance in the modern world, or is it simply a nineteenth-century anachronism? In organising your revision of this topic, you need to make sure that you understand and can discuss the following themes:

1. The conceptual basis of the theory.
2. The simple two crop application.
3. More complex applications and the influence of additional variables.
4. Aspects of modern agricultural production which reduce the validity of the model.
5. Contemporary examples which demonstrate the survival of at least some degree of concentric zonation of agricultural production.

Answer

Guidance notes

Johann Heinrich von Thünen's theory was one of the earliest attempts to explain agricultural land use patterns. It was partly based on his own observations of land use patterns on the North German plain near Mecklenburg where he owned a large estate. His ideas first appeared in his book *Der Isolierte Staat* which was published in 1826. The theory was based on the concept of 'Economic Rent', an idea first described by the economist David Ricardo in 1817, although von Thünen appears to have reached similar conclusions quite independently.

Economic Rent may be defined as the return or profit which can be obtained from any area above that obtainable from land at the margin of production. Ricardo envisaged that Economic Rent would decline as one moved further away from some central city. This was based upon an assumed decrease in soil fertility. However, von Thünen interpreted the same decline as a result of the increase in transport costs with distance from the

The opening paragraph is used to place von Thünen's work in context; that is to say, when and where his ideas were formulated. It is important to establish this information in a question about the contemporary relevance of the theory.

The concept of Economic Rent is central to the theory. In this paragraph it is briefly defined. A simple application of the concept then follows, involving just two crops.

city. In addition, some crops might be bulkier or deteriorate more rapidly and would be more costly to transport than others. Thus, he was able to identify the most profitable crop at any given distance from the central city.

Although a diagram is included, a brief description of what it shows is also considered relevant. You should use diagrams as a substitute for lengthy written description. When you include a diagram, keep the written comments short. Sometimes just a caption under the diagram will suffice.

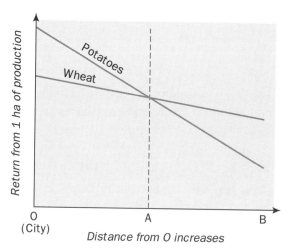

Figure 1 Economic Rent for two crops, potatoes and wheat, taking into account differences in transport costs

The diagram shows the relative profitability of two crops, potatoes and wheat. Potatoes yield a larger bulk per hectare than wheat and are more costly to transport. The profit from potatoes, therefore, shows a steeper decline away from the city market than that of wheat. Under these circumstances, potatoes will be grown between O and A and wheat between A and B. The principle may be applied to any number of crops. By rotating the axis OAB through 360° a concentric pattern of crop zones around the city will result.

von Thünen applied these ideas to an imaginary territory which he described as his '**isolated state**'. He made a number of assumptions about this idealised territory. Physical conditions, such as climate, relief and soil, would be uniform (forming a so-called 'Isotropic Plain'); the state would be surrounded by an uncultivated wilderness and would have no connections with the outside world; all produce would be sold in a single central city; there would be a single mode of transport only (in von Thünen's day, horse-drawn carts) and transport costs would be directly proportional to distance.

Applying his theory to this hypothetical territory, von Thünen described the following sequence of concentric land use zones (from centre to periphery): market gardening, silviculture (timber production), intensive crop production, mixed farming with the emphasis on dairying, a three-field system of mixed farming and finally extensive cattle ranching. Next, two variables were introduced, a navigable river providing transportation and a second city providing an alternative market.

These additional variables were shown to produce distortions to the basic concentric arrangement (see Figure 2).

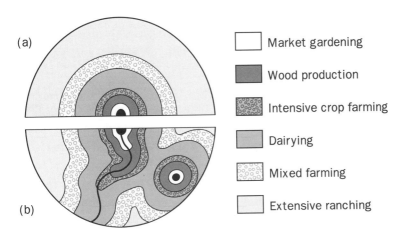

Figure 2 (a) Concentric land use zones in von Thünen's isolated state; (b) land use modified by the introduction of two variables

Many **criticisms** have been levelled against von Thünen's model in recent years. It has been dismissed by some as over-simplistic, anachronistic and of little relevance to contemporary agricultural economics. In support of this claim, mention is usually made of von Thünen's reference to horse-drawn carts as the principle mode of transport, as well as his description of timber production close to the city for purposes of fuel. More importantly, transportation has changed so radically that the very basis of the model is undermined. For example, milk is brought to London daily by rail from Devon and Cornwall, vegetables are flown to the UK from Africa, and meat brought from the southern hemisphere in refrigerated ships.

Further criticisms have focused their attention on the excessively hypothetical nature of the model. There are too many assumptions which can never be fulfilled in reality; for example, the concept of an isotropic surface, and the closed economic system of the isolated state beyond which neither trade nor transport will extend. In addition, there is no reference to the scale of the model. Not surprisingly, there are few perfect examples of von Thünen's concentric land use pattern.

Modern critics have also attacked the theory because of its assumption that all farmers have complete knowledge and will use this perfect knowledge to make rational decisions. In reality, neither assumption is correct, and recent years have witnessed an increasing interest in this behavioural element. Alternative approaches challenge von Thünen's multitude of assumptions, generalisations and simplifications. Game Theory applied by P. Gould considers the problems of decision-making which face the farmer. It recognises the risk involved in deciding which crops to grow, and attempts to show how to minimise this.

Having described and explained the theory, the evaluation starts here. In this paragraph some examples are given of the processes which have undermined the validity of the model.

This paragraph serves two functions in the answer. First, it identifies certain simplistic generalisations implicit in the model. Secondly, it relates von Thünen's ideas to other, more modern, techniques of agricultural land use analysis. While the latter is not essential, this additional insight would distinguish a good answer.

T. Hägerstrand devised a simulation model to explore the uneven diffusion of innovations among farmers. In so doing, he demonstrated that the concept of 'perfect knowledge' was quite unrealistic. At about the same time, J.C. Weaver developed the technique of Crop Combination Analysis, which dismissed the simplistic notion of single crop regions as in the von Thünen model.

However, despite the numerous criticisms which have been levelled at von Thünen's work, his theory cannot be totally dismissed. It represents a unique attempt to provide a theoretical rationale for agricultural land use patterns. While perfect concentric patterns of single crop types fail to exist in reality, many areas show patterns of land use which approximate to the von Thünen model. Concentric arrangements of land use have been described around many Mediterranean villages, and, on a larger scale, the agricultural zones found in Argentina and Uruguay have been analysed in terms of the von Thünen model with distortions caused by the regional distribution of population, settlements, communications and other particular factors. The modern tendency for market gardening and dairying activities to locate around large cities can also be explained in terms of the model.

Like many other geographical models, von Thünen's model is still useful as a measure of comparison. By suggesting the spatial pattern which might be expected on an isotropic surface, it becomes possible to identify the special circumstances which operate to cause distortions to that pattern in the real world. In essence, the model is concerned with the effects of transport costs on profitability and patterns of production. It has been said that 'while transport costs continue to form a major part of the total costs of producing and marketing crops, at least some semblance of a concentric zonal system will remain'.

> This paragraph contains the counter-arguments. The continued existence of concentric or modified-concentric cropping zones suggests that the theory may still have some relevance. This provides you with an opportunity to mention examples that you have read about or studied in class.

> In this final paragraph a judgement is made. The model still has some limited contemporary relevance. This is not a definitive conclusion. You could argue the case differently and still gain a good mark for your answer.

General Comments

If your examination includes a section on data-response questions, then be prepared for von Thünen to turn up there. It is even possible that the examiners might provide a map which shows the pattern of agricultural production in one particular country or region, and ask for its analysis in terms of the von Thünen model.

Related questions

1 What factors influence farmers' choice of crops and livestock in Britain today?

2 Discuss the view that 'von Thünen's model is simply a reflection of the time and place in which it was produced and has no general application'.

Question 25

Describe the effects of large-scale mining and quarrying activities on the landscape.

This question, like several others in this collection, is concerned with the impacts of human activity on the natural environment. The 'task-word' is describe. Generally, these are the easiest and most straightforward questions that you are likely to encounter. On the other hand, although the question is conceptually simple, there is an implicit requirement that your description should contain plenty of detailed factual information, and should refer to a wide range of well-chosen examples.

The sample answer focuses on the UK, but that is not a requirement of the question. You could draw material from any region that you have studied in detail. This answer makes reference to a dozen or more locations where environmental damage is evident. It refers to various government surveys and reports, and quotes from three different authors on the subject. It is that sort of detail that distinguishes a good answer. Solid revision and preparation are essential if you are to have such information at your disposal in the exam.

Answer

Reference to the problems of generalising about very different types of activity makes a good, strong introduction.

The effects of large-scale mining and quarrying activities on the landscape are extremely varied. This is a reflection of the large number of factors involved. Different types of mine — opencast, adit or shaft — impose different requirements on the land; different types of mineral ore generate different volumes and types of waste; different mining companies vary in their attitudes towards the environment: some operate responsibly and with respect for the environment, others are little better than vandals. Given all of this, it is difficult to make broad generalisations about the environmental effects of mineral extraction. In a sense, each mine or quarry is unique, and its environmental impact is particular to its own specific operation.

The environmental impact of mineral extraction is closely tied up with questions of land dereliction. Any discussion of derelict land is immediately hampered by problems of definition which involve both economic and aesthetic considerations. K.L. Wallwork has pointed out that 'it is possible for land to appear to be spoiled and degraded without it being economically derelict...conversely, land which is economically derelict may give no offence to the eye'. In the UK, the official definition (used since 1964 when local authorities were first obliged to compile annual returns of derelict land) is as follows: 'Derelict land is land so damaged by industrial and other development that it is incapable of beneficial use without further treatment.' On this basis, approximately 120,000 ha of land in the UK are officially defined as derelict, although experts are unanimously agreed that this is an understatement of the true situation.

The main causes of land dereliction include mineral extraction and processing, various categories of manufacturing and their related dumping of solid and liquid wastes, abandonment of urban and industrial buildings and transport installations, and the dumping of urban domestic waste. Of these, mining and quarrying are by far the largest contributors to the growing amount of derelict, degraded land. A survey by the Department of the Environment in 1974 revealed 57,000 ha of derelict mineral land and abandoned mine working in England alone. The impact of mining and quarrying on the landscape will be considered under five headings: scarification of the land, waste dumping, surface subsidence, environmental pollution, and the abandonment of buildings and machinery. Each will be examined with reference to examples from the UK.

Scarification of the land refers to the creation of surface pits, holes and depressions as a direct result of mineral extraction. These vary enormously in size and depth. The most common cause of shallow surface depressions is the sand and gravel industry which, depending on the depth of the water-table in relation to the workings, produces either wet or dry pits when extraction is complete. To the west of London, sand and gravel working has created a chain of man-made lakes along the Colne Valley between Rickmansworth and Denham. Similar conditions have been created by sand and gravel workings along the Lea Valley to the north of London. Deeper depressions result from the opencast working of coal, iron-ore, limestone and chalk, and brick-clay. 'The modern dragline excavators used in opencast coal mining can move 1,500 tonnes of material an hour and seek out coal seams 150 m down. In the Bedfordshire brickfield, massive "walking" excavators dig to depths of 30 m, producing immense pits known in the trade as "knottholes", their floors rippled with man-made hills and dales.' (J. Barr, *Derelict Britain*)

The difficulties of defining derelict, damaged and degraded land provide another useful context for the more detailed material which follows.

The plan for the essay is set out here. The five key themes are then 'picked off', paragraph by paragraph. It can be useful for the reader if the plan for the essay is identified in advance.

Five well-selected examples of scarification are integrated into the paragraph.

The worst landscape scars from workings on this scale have resulted from ironstone workings on the Jurassic outcrop of the east Midlands, and brick-clay workings on the Oxford Clay outcrop near Peterborough and Bedford. The deepest mining scars on the landscape result from the working of 'hard' rock such as slate and limestone. For example, the disused Dinorwic slate quarry in north Wales covers 300 ha of mountainside and has left a succession of quarry faces which rise more than 500 m from the floor of the quarry. In a similar manner, the Peak District north of Buxton has been, and continues to be, devastated by a series of gigantic limestone quarries.

Alongside the pits and depressions are the spoil heaps and tailings, the accumulated **waste** of years of mining and quarrying. In the case of opencast working, the **overburden**, which has to be stripped off to reach the mineral being sought, may be piled alongside the working to await replacement when mining is complete. In the case of shaft and adit mines, large volumes of rock waste may be removed and dumped in order to gain access to economically valuable minerals. The waste from coal mines has two main components; rock brought to the surface from the sinking of shafts and the cutting of roadways and tunnels, and waste residues separated out from saleable coal. It has been estimated that 30–35% of the tonnage raised in British coal mines is waste. This is usually dumped adjacent to the pithead. Prior to the Mines and Quarries Act of 1969 (passed in response to the Aberfan disaster of 1966) most waste was dumped in the form of conical or ridge tips, often more than 50 m high; since 1969, it has been spread in the form of low plateau-like surfaces rarely rising above 15 m.

Separation of ore from **gangue minerals** can also generate enormous quantities of waste. The china-clay workings of Cornwall produce 9 tonnes of waste for each tonne of usable china-clay extracted. China-clay waste covers an area of 35 km^2 in the vicinity of St Austell. The tailings of abandoned tin mines in Cornwall and the lead rakes in Derbyshire testify to similar processes. To avoid unnecessary transport costs, low grade metal ores are frequently smelted at the point of extraction, thereby creating further waste for dumping. At the peak of the iron industry of the Black Country in the west Midlands, more than 180 blast furnaces were at work, and an enormous quantity of furnace slag resembling volcanic lava was dumped over the landscape. Similar dumping of copper slag took place along the Lower Swansea Valley in South Wales.

Many types of mining activity produce **surface subsidence** of the land. Strictly speaking, the term 'subsidence' refers to vertical displacement of the surface, but this is usually accompanied by horizontal displacement too. The amount of surface subsidence is related to the volume and thickness of material

Again, a good range of examples of waste dumping are mentioned.

extracted, the method of mining, the nature of the overlying rocks, and the depth of the mine. At the surface, it causes damage to buildings (often necessitating demolition), may disrupt and modify surface drainage patterns, and, most commonly, produces shallow depressions ('flashes') which become permanently flooded. Such features are found in most coalfield areas in Britain. Another well-known example is the salt-mining area of the Weaver Valley in Cheshire where brine-pumping has created numerous subsidence lakes or meres around Northwich, Middlewich and Winsford.

The meres of Cheshire provide a well-known example of surface subsidence. They are described in many texts on geomorphology.

Certain types of mining and quarrying and related ore-processing industries can be potent sources of **pollution**. Opencast working often creates dust and dirt which settles downwind of the site, destroying vegetation. Percolation of water through mining tailings and mounds of furnace slag (which stubbornly resist colonisation by vegetation) can pollute both ground water and surface streams with a variety of chemical toxins. Mines can also introduce inert suspended matter into rivers, as in Cornwall where the hydraulic process of china-clay extraction results in rivers flowing milky-white because of suspended china-clay. The main landscape effect of pollution involves the disruption of natural habitats, especially by damage and destruction of vegetation.

It is a feature of extractive industry that it produces rapid landscape changes. It has been remarked that 'the essential characteristic of mineral exploitation is that it fixes man's labours suddenly, but for the time being only, at one particular place on the earth's surface'. (J. Brunhes) However brief the period of mining activity, termination leaves a landscape littered with **derelict buildings and plant**. 'Former mining areas are disfigured with derelict mining gear and processing machinery, abandoned buildings, disused mineral lines, and associated dirt and rubbish. It is a scene repeated countless times in countless places in old, tired industrial parts of Britain, marred by the freakish hardware left behind when man moves on.' (J. Barr)

The theme of derelict plant and buildings is made by means of two quotations rather than by reference to specific examples. This is quite effective, and provides a contrast with the preceding paragraphs which are rather thick with examples.

It is clear that mining and quarrying activities can produce rapid and substantial landscape changes. The scale of that change has increased over the years in response to the use of increasingly powerful mining and earth-moving equipment. Almost all of these human changes to the landscape are undesirable, and most are unnecessary. The knowledge and techniques of land restoration after mining are well-known, but costly. Some of the worst ravages have been reduced by recent legislation, which requires guarantees of restoration as a condition of granting permission to mine. This, of course, does nothing to remedy the inherited problems of mining dereliction and, in any case, the amount of derelict land in Britain still continues to increase by 1,400 ha per year.

The conclusion draws together points made in the answer, and emphasises the continuing nature of the problem.

Traditionally, questions in economic geography were predominantly about the factors of production. Questions on mining and quarrying usually involved consideration of the nature of the mineral deposit (depth, quality, size of reserve, etc.), production costs (plant, machinery, labour, etc.), location of markets, mode and costs of transportation to market, and so on. The focus was very much on the purely economic aspects of production. Very often the task was to argue the advantage of one location over another. Questions of that type are still set, but less frequently, so you can't afford to neglect the traditional approach entirely. Increasingly, questions in economic geography are concerned with the impacts of production on the physical environment. Impact studies also involve consideration of the legacy of former production.

Related questions

1 With reference to specific localities, examine the problems caused by large-scale sand and gravel extraction. What can be done to restore such areas when extraction ceases?

2 Identify and describe the economic, social and environmental problems which characterise former coal-mining towns and pit villages in the UK.

3 Assess the various ways in which mining and quarrying activities contribute to the pollution of both surface and ground water supplies.

Question 26

With reference to any one country, discuss the factors which encourage the large-scale production of hydro-electric power.

Tackling the question

This is a very straightforward question involving a discussion of the factors favouring or stimulating large-scale hydro-electric power production in a country of your own choice. Those factors will, of course, include both physical and economic considerations. Make sure that you don't limit the discussion simply to physical factors. The compilation of such an inventory should present few problems. However, because it is such an easy question, it does raise an important point: how can you make your answer stand out as better than average? Probably the best way of achieving that is by demonstrating a detailed knowledge of your selected country. Ideally, you should include precipitation statistics, names of specific rivers used for HEP production, names of actual power schemes, HEP production statistics, and possibly even a sketch-map showing the location of features mentioned in your answer. By demonstrating that sort of detailed knowledge your answer will stand out from the rest. In other words, you require some really good case-study material.

Any of the leading HEP producers — Canada, USA, Russia, Norway, Sweden, Switzerland, France, etc. — would provide plenty of discussion points and make a suitable choice for your answer. For this particular essay, Norway has been selected.

Answer

Guidance notes

Norway is a country which clearly illustrates the wide range of factors that encourage the large-scale production of hydro-electric power (HEP). In 1990, Norway ranked fourth among the world's producers of HEP, its output of almost 105,000 million kWh being exceeded only by Canada, the USA and the former USSR. However, compared with these other nations, Norway has only a very small population, a mere 4.1 million and, as a result, has the highest per capita production of HEP in the world. HEP accounts for 99% of the electricity generated in Norway. As elsewhere, the factors which have encouraged the successful large-scale development of HEP in Norway fall into two clear categories, physical and economic.

The chosen country is identified at the outset — first word of the first paragraph. The alternative is to preface your essay with a heading — hydro-electric power production in Norway.

Obviously, it saves a great deal of time to use abbreviations and acronyms, but names and terms should be written in full on the first occasion that they appear.

This and the following two paragraphs cover the physical conditions which favour hydro-electrical power production.

Try to include this level of detail in your answers; mention actual rivers with major power stations. This type of detail characterises the best answers.

Any nation intending to develop HEP must be able to satisfy the various **physical requirements**. Norway has the advantage of high **mountainous relief**, with peaks reaching over 2,000 m in the southern part of the country. There are numerous rivers capable of producing the necessary **head of water** for HEP production. In the fjord country of West Norway, small mountain streams fall through great heights in a relatively short distance, while in the south and east of the country there are many large rivers, such as the Glåma and Lågen which flow with relatively gentle gradients towards Oslo Fjord and the Skagerrak. Both types of river offer possibilities for HEP production, since the necessary head of water may result from either a small volume of water with a large fall or a large volume of water with a relatively small fall.

The former **glaciation** of Norway has also created suitable conditions for HEP production. In the west, the high **waterfalls** are often associated with hanging valleys while, in the south and east, the smaller falls and rapids can often be related to the stepped long profile of glaciated valleys or knickpoints resulting from the post-glacial rejuvenation of river systems due to isostatic uplift. Glacial erosion has also exposed areas of **bare rock** and solid geology. This facilitates engineering work, providing, in particular, the best possible conditions for the construction of large retaining dams. Narrow, steep-sided, U-shaped, **glaciated valleys** also facilitate dam construction compared with broad V-shaped valleys with a deep infill of sedimentary material. Glaciation has also produced large numbers of **lakes** in Norway. Many occupy ice-eroded basins or have collected behind moraine barriers. Whatever their mode of formation, they have the effect of regulating river flow and reducing the highs and lows of seasonal discharge.

Other physical factors which have encouraged HEP production in Norway are largely climatic. **Precipitation** is moderate to high, ranging from a modest 500 mm per year along the border with Sweden to over 2,500 mm per year in the mountainous districts of the west. Most importantly, in the context of HEP production, precipitation is distributed fairly evenly throughout the year, although some eastern districts do experience a slight summer maximum. River discharge in late spring and early summer is augmented by melting snow in the mountains. **Evaporation rates** are generally low in Norway and indirectly help to increase the flow of surface water.

Economic factors are introduced here. The two sets of factors, physical and economic, are given roughly equal weight in the essay.

In addition to these physical factors, Norway also illustrates a number of **economic factors** which have encouraged the large-scale development of HEP resources. To a large extent, physical factors determine the HEP potential of any nation, while economic factors are responsible for the translation of that potential into actual production. Norway's development, as one of the world's leading producers of HEP, is closely linked with the processes of urbanisation and industrialisation which have transformed the economy and society of the country during the present century. For example, during the 1950s Norway experienced a period of rapid industrial growth which coincidentally was also a period of enormous increase in HEP production capacity. It is fortunate that the best sites for HEP production are located in the south of the country where the centres of greatest demand are also found e.g. Oslo, Bergen, Stavanger, Trondheim, Kristiansand, etc. Centres of demand must be located within the radius over which power may be economically transported. Until recently, that radius was approximately 350 km, but recent developments in power transmission technology have increased the distance over which electricity may be economically cabled. In Norway, the greatest concentration of large HEP stations is in the south-east of the country, for example, in Telemark, close to the main centres of population and economic activity.

Until recently, Norwegian HEP development could be explained in terms of a lack of **alternative energy supplies**. Norway's only coal field lies on the remote Arctic island of Spitsbergen. In recent years, the Norwegian sector of the North Sea has yielded enormous quantities of oil and gas. However, Norway has exported most of its North Sea oil and gas, partly because of the difficulties of constructing pipelines to the Norwegian coast due to the presence of a deep off-shore trench, and partly in order to generate capital for investment in infrastructure improvements and additional HEP plant. This is a recognition of the fact that North Sea oil and gas will eventually be exhausted, whereas investment in a renewable energy source is an investment for the future. Oil and gas revenues have provided the capital needed for the extremely high cost of constructing retaining dams, power stations and transmission lines.

Although Norway provides almost ideal conditions for HEP development, it should not be assumed that HEP production is without its **problems**. Parts of north Norway have extensive plateau areas which are less than ideal for HEP schemes. From time to time, Norway experiences low rainfall conditions which reduce power production. Fortunately, the establishment of NORDEL, an organisation concerned with energy exchanges among the Scandinavian nations, has reduced the impact of low production periods. Winter freezing of rivers and lakes can reduce discharge of some rivers at a time when demand for electricity is greatest. During periods of intense winter cold, the accumulation of frost on power lines can cause their collapse. The construction of transmission lines is, of course, very difficult and costly over mountainous terrain with deep valleys and wide fjords.

Some of the problems and conflicts resulting from hydro-electrical power production are identified in these final two paragraphs. Although these points are not specifically requested in the question, their inclusion creates a more balanced answer.

As well as physical problems, there are economic difficulties too, in particular the **conflict** between HEP production and other sectors of the economy. The flooding of valleys to create reservoirs is in direct conflict with the demands of tourism. The diversion of rivers formerly used for timber floating may be in conflict with the interests of the timber industry. The flooding of grazing land may cause hardship to farmers. One example of such conflict emerged in 1979 when details were announced of a proposed HEP project which would have involved flooding sections of the Alta Valley in northern Norway. This would have disrupted traditional migration routes for reindeer and their Lappish herders. A well-organised protest movement with the slogan *'elva skal leve'* (the river shall live) eventually led to the abandonment of this particular proposal. Although the benefits of HEP to Norway are enormous, it is also clear that the Norwegian people do not want HEP at any cost. Beneficial and detrimental effects must be carefully evaluated.

General comments

An important theme in modern geography is that of 'sustainability'. Some exam boards even have a section of the A-level syllabus devoted to the subject. Sustainable development involves a search for new, alternative strategies for social and economic development, strategies which consume less of the earth's non-renewable resources, show more respect and sensitivity for the global environment, and cause less environmental damage. Comparisons of different sources of fuel and power could easily be embedded into the sustainability theme. Hydro-electric power, the subject of this essay, is arguably less environmentally friendly than, say, wind power, but is also a good deal cleaner than power derived from the burning of fossil fuels.

Related questions

1 With reference to a range of examples, analyse the factors which determine the energy-mix of particular countries.

2 Explain why hydro-electric power production makes only a relatively small contribution to total electric power generation in the UK.

3 Hydro-electric power production is dominated by the developed nations of the world. Suggest why the potential for hydro-electric power production in the developing nations remains relatively unexploited.

Question 27

Why do many industries occupy sub-optimal locations?

Tackling the question

Questions on industrial location frequently require a discussion of various models and theories of location, together with some reference to real-world examples to illustrate the principles involved. This question is typical of what you might expect, although in this case there is no specific, stated requirement to refer to actual industries occupying sub-optimal locations.

This is a very open question. It gives you the opportunity to approach the question in a number of different ways. You could, for example, put the emphasis on two or three case studies of actual industries occupying sub-optimal locations, and then draw some general themes and principles from those carefully selected examples. The sample answer adopts a more theoretical approach. It is essentially a review of ideas about optimum and sub-optimum locations in the context of the development of industrial location theory. Either approach, empirical or theoretical, is equally valid.

Answer

In the context of industrial location theory, the concept of optimum location implies that there is, for each industry, a single best location. The question then arises as to what is meant by 'best' or 'optimum location', since the term can be interpreted in economic or social or political ways. However, since location theory has been largely developed in capitalist societies, the best location is generally assumed to be that which yields the **highest profits**. The best location for any industry, therefore, is where the difference between revenues and costs is greatest, since income minus expenditure equals profit.

However, in recent years, the assumption that actual decisions are made simply on the basis of **profit-maximisation** has been called into question. There is now a greater awareness that decisions about industrial location may be based upon goals other than that of making money. Governments, for example, may be satisfied to establish new industry in sub-optimal

Guidance notes

Problems relating to the concept of optimum location are used as an introduction to the topic before moving on to a discussion of sub-optimal locations.

Early views about optimum location are reviewed in this paragraph. This provides you with an opportunity to demonstrate your awareness of important early contributors to the debate — Weber, Hoover, Hotelling, Lösch, etc.

locations in order to combat high unemployment or to achieve other social or strategic objectives. In any case, there are two serious problems to be faced in the development of profit-maximisation theories of industrial location. First, such locations are difficult to find due to the large number of variables which affect both costs and revenues. Secondly, profitability is not absolute, and a distinction has to be made between short-term and long-term profitability. That is to say, the maximum-profit location of today almost certainly will not be the maximum-profit location of tomorrow.

Because of the practical problems involved in developing maximum-profit theories, two principal approaches have been adopted which examine the questions of costs and revenues separately. In the first approach, the so-called **least-cost theories**, revenues are taken to be equal at all locations, but costs are assumed to vary from place to place. The search, therefore, is to find the point of minimum production costs. This is then taken to be the optimum location. Typical of this approach is the work of A. Weber (1909), T. Pallander (1935) and E. Hoover (1937), all of whom were more concerned with cost than the demand factor. In the second approach, the so-called **maximum-revenue theories**, production costs are taken to be equal at all locations, and variations in market demand and revenue are examined. The point of maximum revenue is assumed to be the optimum location. This latter approach is typified by the work of H. Hotelling (1929) and A. Lösch (1954). Of course, the least-cost school has not totally ignored revenues, nor has the maximum-revenue school totally ignored costs, but each has placed a distinct emphasis on one aspect or the other. What this means is that any optimum location produced by either approach is based upon an inadequate consideration of either cost or revenue. For this and other reasons, the search for a single best location has largely been abandoned in recent years. It is difficult, if not impossible, to locate, and, even if it could be located, its position changes in response to economic circumstances. It also implies that only one firm can occupy the optimum location, and that all others must therefore operate from sub-optimal locations.

The shift away from a search for a single best location to the identification of parameters within which firms can make a profit is mentioned next. This starts to lock the answer firmly into the question.

The emphasis in industrial location theory has shifted away from the search for an optimum location to the identification of the **margin of profitability** within which any firm must operate if it is to conduct a profitable business. The concept was first discussed by E.M. Rawstron in 1958 when he demonstrated that firms can make profits and stay in business without necessarily finding the optimum location. Rawstron argued that 'it is impossible for a firm ever to know whether it is at the optimum, but its profit and loss account would soon indicate whether it was located beyond the margin'. The concept of the margin of profitability was elaborated upon by D.M. Smith in his book *Industrial Location* (1971).

In Figure 1, both cost and price (revenue) are shown to vary spatially in a section across a given area. Between M_a and M_b price exceeds costs, and a profit will be made. Beyond the margins of profitability, costs exceed price, and a loss will be incurred. O is the maximum-profit or optimum location. The diagram reveals very clearly how and why factories occupy sub-optimal locations. Provided that they are located within the margins, they can carry out a profitable business. 'The concept of the margin creates a dynamic space within which economically sub-optimal locational decision-making by firms can be accommodated.' (B.W. Hodder and R. Lee)

Smith's work on 'margins of profitability' is an essential element in the answer.

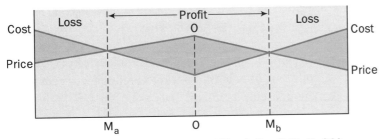

Figure 1 The margins of profitability (after D.M. Smith)

Sub-optimal locations of factories might be the result of decisions based on **imperfect knowledge** about the factors of production and market demand, or decisions based on the **poor use of good information** by weak, ineffectual management. Considerations such as these, which are typical of the behavioural approach to industrial location, have been examined by A. Pred (1967) by means of a behavioural matrix. Figure 2 represents the basis on which six locational decisions have been made. Two factories occupy optimum locations. Three occupy sub-optimal locations within the margin of profitability, and one occupies a sub-optimal location outside the margin of profitability.

Similarly, the behavioural approach to decision-making developed by Pred provides another important element of a good answer. It serves as a reminder that the quality of information on which decisions are based and the ability of decision-makers to use information are important considerations.

Manager 1   has made the right decision by using good information wisely.

Manager 2   is in a similar location purely by chance.

Manager 3   is like Manager 2, but less lucky. The company is making no profit and will go out of business soon.

Manager 4   is making a profit, but not doing as well as possible, because information has not been used wisely.

Manager 5   is in a similar position to Manager 4, but for different reasons. Although competent, the supply of information is poor.

Manager 6   is making a reasonable profit with moderately good information and moderate ability.

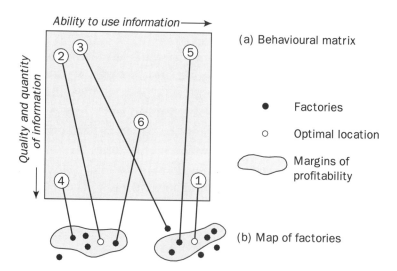

Figure 2 Industrial location decisions linked to a behavioural matrix (after A. Pred)

The behavioural approach to locational decision-making serves to remind us of two different interpretations of economic activities. The first views industrialists as **optimisers** seeking to achieve maximum returns for their endeavours but constrained by imperfect information and limited ability. The other view sees industrialists as **satisficers**, happy to accept sub-optimal locations with which they are nevertheless satisfied. The latter view suggests that locational factors (such as attractive environment, congenial climate, pleasant working conditions and so on) may be just as important as profit-maximisation.

Behavioural theory also serves to remind us of the unpredictability of human behaviour and the fact that many industrial location decisions are made for the most unlikely and irrational reasons. Many major industries are found in sub-optimal locations for no better reason than they just happen to be the birthplace of the founder of the company or the place where a particular industrial technique was first developed. These are the sole reasons for the location of the motor industry in Oxford, the pharmaceutical and tobacco industries in Nottingham, the pottery industry in Stoke-on-Trent and the knitwear and lace industries in the East Midlands. Clearly, then, there are many reasons why factories may occupy sub-optimal locations: inertia, ignorance, inability, error, choice, whim and chance, to name but a few.

Finally, the fact that many locational decisions are illogical and irrational is developed in this paragraph. Key points made in the body of the essay are tightly summarised in the final sentence of the answer.

General Comments

The principles and theories used to explain the location of manufacturing industry constitute a popular topic with examiners. You need to be familiar with the main theoretical approaches and the key contributors to the debate. You should be able to comment on least-cost theories, maximum-revenue theories, ideas about the margins of profitability, and the application of a behavioural approach to explain locational decision-making. There are some important diagrams related to this subject area. You might consider learning them so that you can reproduce them in the exam if necessary. Be aware too that the models of Weber and Smith are used from time to time as the basis for data-response questions.

Related questions

1   Describe and explain the distribution of manufacturing industry in any one large city that you have studied or know well.

2   With reference to actual examples, describe and explain what is meant by the term 'industrial inertia'.

3   Discuss the problems involved in identifying the optimum location for any manufacturing industry.

What is a town? Discuss the problems involved in the definition of urban settlements.

Tackling the question

This question is all about problems of definition and terminology. How can precision and universality of meaning be attached to terms which are simultaneously part of the vocabulary of geography and also part of everyday, non-specialist language and conversation? Specifically, how can we distinguish precisely between urban and rural? Where exactly is the defining boundary to be drawn between these contrasting settlement forms? Is it possible to quantify the terms town and country?

You could attempt an answer which embodies your own thoughts on these questions, but it would probably be quite restricted in scope and length. A more productive approach is to compare and evaluate the definitions used by various writers on the subject and employed in census reports and other official documentation. It is this latter approach which has been used in the sample answer.

Answer

This is a short, concise quotation which sums up the problem very neatly. It also 'flags' various themes which will be picked up later on in the essay.

From this point onwards, various criteria which might provide a basis

What is a town? Initially, this appears to be a naive and simple question. One assumes that everyone knows exactly what constitutes a town, and could differentiate between town and village settlements. It is this general familiarity which is at the heart of the problem of defining urban settlements. There is an enormous range of subjective opinion and impression, when what is required is a precise, objective definition of the nature and characteristics of urban settlements. In fact, the town defies simple definition. Emrys Jones has commented on this point: 'Is it [the town] a physical conglomeration of streets and houses, or is it a centre of exchange and commerce? Or is it a kind of society, or even a frame of mind? Has it a certain size, a specific density? The difficulties in definition are countless, and there is very little unanimity: it seems to be all things to all men.' Not surprisingly, therefore, a wide variety of criteria have been employed by administrators, planners and researchers in the search for a satisfactory definition.

One obvious method is to define towns in terms of a **minimum population size**. Several countries employ this method for the compilation of their published statistics on the relative sizes of their urban and rural populations. Unfortunately, there is no general consensus on the selected minimum figure. Norway, for example, defines a town as 'a settlement agglomeration with a minimum of 200 inhabitants'. In the Netherlands, urban settlements are defined as 'municipalities with a population of 2,000 or more inhabitants'. In Japan, towns must have at least 50,000 inhabitants, together with certain other economic characteristics. Clearly, any published statistics about the size or proportion of urban population in any country must be treated with caution. It would be quite meaningless, for example, to compare statistics for the proportion of urban population in Norway and Japan, given that their definitions of 'urban' differ so radically.

An essential feature of towns is their high density of population. Compared with rural settlements, towns and cities are characterised by a high concentration of workers and residents within relatively small areas. This is especially true of inner city areas where nineteenth-century tenements and closely packed terraced housing, together with recently constructed high-rise buildings, can create exceptionally high densities of population. It is reasonable to suppose, therefore, that this essential urban characteristic might provide a basis for definition. A few countries do make reference to **population density** as part of their definition of towns. In Canada, for example, an officially designated town must have a minimum population of 1,000 together with a population density which reaches at least 1,000 persons per square mile or 390 persons per square kilometre. India also employs the same density figure in its definition of urban settlements. However, absolute numbers, whether population size or density, do not provide a wholly satisfactory means of definition. Small settlements may display all the economic and social characteristics of towns, while settlements of considerable size, especially in the Third World, may contain a large proportion of agricultural workers and display essentially rural characteristics.

As an alternative to size and density figures, some authorities take **settlement functions** into account. Towns are generally regarded as settlements in which the majority of workers have been released from the primary task of food production, and engage in secondary and tertiary trades and activities. Thus, a true urban settlement might be expected to contain relatively few agricultural workers, but many workers in the manufacturing and service sectors. Officially defined towns in India, as well as fulfilling certain conditions of size and density, must additionally have 'at least 75% of the adult male population in pursuits other than agriculture'. Similarly, in the Netherlands, towns must have 'no more than 20% of the economically

for definition are introduced. This sequence of points, one per paragraph, starts with the notion of minimum population size.

Population density is considered here. As in the previous paragraph, a number of examples are introduced of countries which use this particular criterion.

Settlement function is now considered as a possible criterion for definition. As with the previous factors, its theoretical potential is considered, examples are given, and problems associated with its use are identified.

active male population engaged in agriculture'. Although functional characteristics provide a reasonably good indicator in the developed nations, they are less satisfactory in the Third World where settlements, which are urban in almost every other respect, often house a very large agrarian population. A further problem with this approach is that it fails to work well when applied historically. Even in the towns of the developed nations, a high level of employment in the secondary and tertiary sectors is a relatively recent phenomenon.

Another criterion which has been employed is the presence of certain typically **urban buildings and other landscape features**, such as a cathedral, university, town-hall or large general hospital. This is a vague, imprecise method which is difficult to apply. A few countries use this approach in combination with other criteria.

Another suggestion is that the essential difference between urban and rural settlements lies in their **sociological characteristics**. This idea was explored as early as 1938 by the American sociologist, Louis Wirth, in a paper entitled 'Urbanism as a Way of Life'. According to Wirth, the social structure of towns and cities is characterised by 'anonymity and lack of personal contact, a weakening of kinship and family ties, and their replacement by allegiance to diverse groups and organisations outside the family....Under these circumstances personal disorganisation, mental breakdown, suicide, delinquency, crime, corruption and disorder are more prevalent in the urban than in the rural community.' One problem with the sociological approach which defines urbanism as 'a way of life' is that it fails to take into account the physical or morphological features of the town itself. Emphasis is placed on the city-dwellers rather than the city itself.

What is a town? Clearly, the question is more difficult to answer than one might suppose. None of the criteria used for definition is without its limitations. Increasingly, the view is expressed that a simple definition of the terms 'urban' and 'rural' is impossible. It is often suggested that, in accordance with the Rank-size Rule, there is, in most countries and regions, a continuum of settlements from largest to smallest, from most important to least important, and that any break or division on that continuum is inevitably subjective and arbitrary.

The use of key indicator buildings is not important. It is mentioned only briefly and allocated a short paragraph.

In contrast, Wirth's ideas on 'Urbanism as a Way of Life' are important. It is unlikely that you will have read his original paper, but you should be familiar with summaries of his ideas.

At the end of the discussion a precise definition still remains elusive. Thus, the suggestion is made that it may be better to think of a continuum of settlements from rural to urban with no clear division between the opposite ends of the settlement scale.

General Comments

One of the skills in writing exam answers is being able to draw material together from several different subject compartments. You need to be able to make connections between different topics, and synthesise material from different sources. The sample answer displays an awareness of the debate about settlement hierarchies. It shows a knowledge of census data. It refers to the differences between towns in developed and developing nations. It makes reference to urban morphology as well as discussing the sociological characteristics of towns. In most textbooks these topics are dispersed through several chapters.

Related questions

1 What are the essential differences between pre-industrial, industrial and post-industrial towns?

2 In what ways do the rapidly growing cities of the Third World differ from those of the developed nations?

3 Schemes to define towns and cities in terms of their social and cultural characteristics inevitably lack precision and are impossible to quantify. Elaborate on this assertion.

(a) Explain the rapid growth of cities in the Third World.

(b) What problems have resulted from that growth?

Tackling the question

Urbanisation in the Third World is a topic which you cannot afford to neglect. Not only do questions on this subject appear with great regularity, but they also tend to focus on a limited number of themes. You need to consider the causes of urbanisation in the Third World, the 'mechanics' of the process, and the results of uncontrolled urban growth. Some questions require that you make reference to a case study of one particular Third World city. Even if not specifically requested, case-study material can provide useful detail and realism to otherwise bland, generalised answers.

This particular question is typical, almost predictable, of what you might expect on this topic. It is a two-part question dealing with the causes and consequences of the urbanisation process in developing nations. In the absence of any mark allocation, the two parts are assumed to carry equal marks, and are given roughly equal length and weight in the answer.

Answer

The introductory paragraph provides a broad setting for the answer. It places contemporary Third World urbanisation in both a temporal and spatial context.

(a) It is a well-known fact that the world's population is becoming increasingly urbanised. Prior to the twentieth century, most of that urban growth was confined to nations such as Great Britain, France, Germany and the United States which had begun to industrialise in the eighteenth and nineteenth centuries. At that time, urban growth in the under-developed nations was relatively slow and modest by comparison. Today that position is reversed. In recent decades, there have been clear signs that urban growth in Europe and North America is slowing down, while at the same time many Third World nations are now displaying rapid and accelerating urban growth. 'In Third World countries the "modern" process of urbanisation is still unfolding. It has some characteristics which relate to the "stage" already experienced by Western societies in the nineteenth century, but is substantially modified by its own cultural contexts and by the fact that it is occurring in a radically different global framework.' (D.T. Herbert and C.J. Thomas)

Different measures may be used to express the degree of urbanisation of a particular country. One method is to consider the percentage of total population living in towns and cities above a certain minimum size, say 50,000 inhabitants. Thus, in Brazil 28% of the total population lived in towns exceeding 50,000 in 1940, and by 1990 that figure had increased to 74%. During the same period, Colombia's urban population rose from 29% to 68% of the national total. Another approach is to use so-called '**million cities**' as indicators of urbanisation. In 1900 there were eleven of these largest cities worldwide, with just a single one (Calcutta) located within the tropics. By 1990 there were 220 'million cities' worldwide, of which 68 were located within the tropics. A closer examination of just five of these 'million cities' reveals alarming rates of growth during the 30-year period from 1960 to 1990.

City	1960	1990	Increase (%)
Mexico City	2,832,000	13,879,000	+ 390.1
São Paulo	3,165,000	11,129,000	+ 251.6
Beijing (Peking)	4,010,000	9,180,000	+ 128.9
Karachi	1,913,000	5,181,000	+ 170.8
Cairo	2,152,000	6,052,000	+ 181.2

Growth of selected urban agglomerations 1960–90

Rapid urban growth in the Third World is the product of two processes. First, a high rate of natural increase of population within the cities themselves. Although death rates are high in most Third World cities, birth rates are even higher, producing a large surplus of births over deaths. Some cities, with better housing and medical services and a generally higher standard of living, have succeeded in reducing their death rate to Western levels or even lower, so that the gap between a high birth rate and low death rate is particularly pronounced. Thus, Singapore has a population of approximately 3 million occupying an area of 581 km^2 to give an average density of more than 5,000 persons per km^2. Its crude birth rate is $21^0/_{00}$ — but its crude death rate is only about half that of the UK — $5.5^0/_{00}$. This gives a natural increase rate of $15.5^0/_{00}$ or 1.55% per year. The second cause of urban growth in the Third World is migration. Third World cities, almost without exception, attract enormous numbers of migrants from their surrounding areas. Although there is some return migration, in-migration far exceeds out-

Two ways of measuring urbanisation are introduced in this paragraph, with useful statistical examples of each measure.

Sizes of the largest urban settlements in individual nations are tabulated in the *United Nations Demographic Yearbooks*. Unfortunately there is a time lag of five years or more between the year of publication and the data contained in a particular yearbook. Although it would be difficult to reproduce such a table in an exam, it is worth learning a few statistics for inclusion in your answer. The figures can be 'rounded'.

The causes of Third World urbanisation are explored in this and the following paragraph. High rates of natural increase and migration into the cities from rural areas are both identified as essential causes.

migration, so that the various cities have a very pronounced positive net migration balance. In Lagos, 75% of the population was born elsewhere and has moved into the city; corresponding figures for São Paulo and Djakarta are 68% and 62% respectively. This combination of natural increase and in-migration produces explosive urban growth.

Given that these cities offer little to the potential migrant by way of housing or employment, it is at first surprising that a flood of population should continue to stream from the rural areas to the cities. Clearly, the attractions of the city are imagined rather than real. Rural problems also help to explain the process. 'Conditions in the countryside are often very bad. Overcrowding, land-fragmentation, over-grazing, soil-erosion, drought, pests, all these ills lead to chronic under-employment and distress, forcing peasants to abandon their plots and move into the towns. Caracas, Rio de Janiero, Brazzaville, Calcutta, Rangoon, Manila...cities such as these become the goals for hundreds of thousands of rural migrants, people without land, jobs, money or possessions, for whom the remote chance of finding an urban occupation is a last remaining hope...they arrive destitute and homeless at their final destination.' (J.H. Lowry)

(b) It is inevitable that the rapid and uncontrolled growth of Third World cities will produce serious economic and social problems. The most obvious of these is **housing**. Large numbers, the so-called street-sleepers, remain homeless and live on the streets. Others become slum tenement dwellers. Many, in the absence of even the most basic permanent accommodation, become squatters in the **shanty towns** which are ubiquitous throughout the Third World. These are the *bidonvilles* of Algiers, the cardboard towns of Khartoum, the *jacoles* of Mexico City, the *favelas* of Rio, the *villas miseria* of Buenos Aires, and so on. More than anything else, they symbolize the failure of the Third World city to deal with the demands placed upon it by rapid population growth. Within the shanty towns there is an absence of even the most basic amenities, such as a piped water-supply and sewage and refuse disposal. The squatter population lives in the most appalling, overcrowded, impoverished conditions. It has been estimated that 44% of the population of Mexico City live in shanty towns; in Rio de Janiero 33%; in Manila 30%, and in São Paulo 18%.

Not surprisingly, **health problems** are particularly serious in Third World cities. Infant mortality is inevitably very high. Polluted water, inadequate sanitation and overcrowding cause outbreaks of cholera and typhoid and the rapid spread of influenza epidemics. High volumes of traffic and growing

Although it may not be possible to produce such a long quotation under exam conditions, sections of it could be memorised and introduced where appropriate.

In the second part of the answer, problems associated with rapid urbanisation are described in a clear, systematic manner; housing, health, unemployment and service provision are allocated one paragraph each.

amounts of industry, combined with lax anti-pollution laws, lead to a high incidence of chronic bronchitis and other respiratory diseases. Added to these are the stress-related illnesses — hypertension, heart disease and mental illness — induced by the routine of survival under the most debased circumstances in what is a strange and alien environment for those newly arrived in the city.

Persistent **high unemployment** is another problem resulting from rapid urban growth in the Third World. In the cities, a fragile industrial economy is in direct competition with Western producers. The number of jobs that industry generates is far exceeded by the number of new arrivals seeking work. D.J. Dwyer has suggested that new industrial projects may even accentuate the problem. 'The increment of employment resulting from such a project may well be accompanied by an increase in unemployment because the new source of wealth attracts such large numbers seeking to obtain benefit from it.' Typically, underemployment abounds alongside unemployment. Large number of street-traders and domestic servants, excessive numbers of office-workers and middlemen in commerce all testify to underemployment just as clearly as the beggars in the street indicate unemployment.

Rapid urban growth also leads to **disruption and near-collapse of urban services**. This may be due in part to maladministration, but is also due to the continually growing demands placed on services already strained close to breaking point. The following comment by J.J. Carroll on urban services in Manila serves to illustrate the point: 'In the past 12 months Manila has had a water shortage in which some 70% of the metropolitan area was without a regular supply...it has had a garbage crisis ...there has been a school crisis...electrical services went through a bad period some months ago...mail is in a continual state of crisis, and in general it seems better to give up trying to use the phone...police and fire protection are unreliable, and the constantly increasing burden of traffic and the condition of the roads discourage one from venturing beyond walking distance.'

These urban problems are not exclusive to Third World cities. It is simply that they are present on a greater scale than in Western cities. Housing is worse, unemployment higher, poverty greater, and pessimism and despair more deep-rooted. The short-term prospects for any significant improvement also seem more remote. Not only is the backlog of inherited problems enormous, but the wave of migrants to the cities continues unabated, thus further adding to the scale of the problems year by year. Acute poverty and deprivation are likely to remain the lot of most city dwellers in the Third World for many generations to come.

The virtual collapse of urban services and infrastructure is described by Carroll. If you have detailed information of this type, try to work it into your answers. It can add style and distinction to your essays. This in turn goes back to the whole process of making notes and preparing for the exam. File cuttings of useful newspaper articles, summarise articles in magazines and periodicals, and make a note of any potentially useful quotations.

General comments

Be prepared for questions on urbanisation which require you to make comparisons and contrasts between the cities of developed and developing nations. As well as economic, social and cultural differences, there are important structural differences. You need to be familiar with the various structural models which have been formulated for both Western and Third World cities. It is not unknown for diagrams of those models to be used for data-response questions.

Related questions

1 Review the various attempts which have been made to devise a structural model for Third World cities.

2 Describe and comment on the typical morphological and social characteristics of shanty towns found in Third World cities.

3 Explain the reasons for the explosive growth of large towns and cities in most developing nations.

Question 30

What is meant by the term 'urban primacy'? Examine the factors which account for variations in urban primacy from one country to another.

Tackling the question

There is a large and important body of geographical literature concerned with the theoretical relationships between urban settlements within regions and nations. Various writers have sought to identify an underlying logic and regularity between towns and cities with respect to their size, spacing and function. There is no requirement for students to refer to the original writings of Christaller (1933), Lösch (1954), Zipf (1949), Jefferson (1939) et al. On the other hand, you are expected to be familiar with the methodology and arguments employed by these key theorists. In other words, a close reading and a clear understanding of the relevant chapters in the standard urban geography textbooks dealing with the Rank-size Rule, urban primacy, central place theory, etc. are essential.

This particular question is concerned solely with the size relationships of towns and cities; specifically, the relationship between the largest and second-largest cities in any country. Don't get drawn into a discussion of central place networks and settlement spacing. That is irrelevant here.

Answer

The Rank-size Rule, proposed by G.K. Zipf in 1949, is concerned with the relationship between city size (population) and city rank (based on a ranking scale from largest to smallest) in any country or region. According to Zipf: 'If all the urban settlements in an area are ranked in descending order of population, the population of the nth town will be 1/nth that of the largest town.' In other words, the population of urban settlements in a region can be arranged in the series 1, 1/2, 1/3, 1/4...1/n. This regularity may also be expressed by the formula,

$$P_n = \frac{P1}{n}$$

Guidance notes

In this opening paragraph the Rank-size Rule is variously presented as a statement, as a numerical series and as an equation. In the final sentence a worked example is also given. This provides the context for the more specific theme of urban primacy which follows.

in which P_n is the population of the town of rank n in the descending order and P1 is the population of the largest city. Thus, if the largest city has a population of 1 million, the 10th ranking city should, according to the rule, have a population of 100,000.

Whereas the Rank-size Rule examines the rank-size relationship between all settlements in a region, urban primacy is concerned specifically with the size relationship between the largest and second-largest cities in any country or region. According to the Rank-size Rule, the largest city, or **primate city** as it is termed, should theoretically be twice the size of the next-largest city. That is to say, the sizes of the largest and next-largest cities should theoretically be in the ratio of 2:1. When that ratio is exceeded and the primate city is more than twice the size of the second city, that country is described as having a **high level of urban primacy**. Conversely, when the ratio is less than 2:1 and the two leading cities are more nearly equal in size, that area is described as having a **low level of urban primacy**. Figure 1 shows hypothetical variations in urban primacy. In the high primacy situation there is a sharp decrease in the sizes of the ten largest cities, while in the low primacy situation the ten largest cities display only relatively small variations in size.

The question is about variations in urban primacy. So, at an early stage in the answer, two common variations from 'normal' primacy are introduced and described. Because these variations — high and low primacy — are central to the question, it is considered worthwhile to present them in diagram form as well.

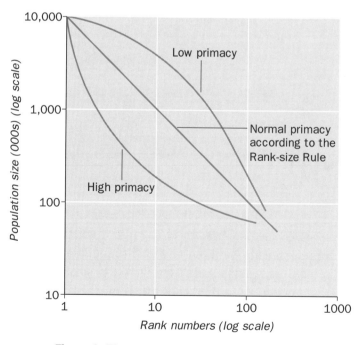

Figure 1 Three types of rank-size relationships

This paragraph provides some actual examples of primacy ratios. You should learn one or two as part of your revision.

In reality, there is an enormous variation in the level of urban primacy from one country to another. For example, Canada demonstrates extremely low primacy; its two largest cities, Toronto and Montreal, have populations of 3,550,000 and

3,021,000 respectively, giving a primacy ratio of virtually 1.18:1. In contrast, Uruguay has a higher level of urban primacy than any other country in the world; its primate city, Montevideo, has a population of 1,450,000 compared with a mere 85,000 in the second city, Paysandu; this gives a primacy ratio of 17:1. Poland conforms to the Rank-size Rule prediction almost perfectly; its two largest cities, Warsaw and Lodz, have populations of 1,675,000 and 852,000 to give a ratio of almost exactly 2:1. The crucial question is, why should these differences exist? What are the causes of variations in urban primacy from one country to another?

An early explanation was offered by **Mark Jefferson**, in his 'Law of the Primate City' published in 1939. Jefferson suggested that, once a particular city starts to become dominant in a country or region, 'that fact alone will give it an impetus to grow that cannot affect any other city, and it draws away from all others in character as well as size to become the primate city'. What Jefferson was describing is the process currently known as cumulative causation. Referring to Denmark, which has a primacy ratio of almost 8:1, he asks, 'Why does the ambitious Dane go to Copenhagen? To attend the university, to study art or music, to write for the press, to attend the museum or theatre, to buy or sell if he has unusual wares or wants unusual wares. Because he keeps hearing and reading of men who live there, men whom he is keen to meet face to face. Perhaps he means to try his wits against them. Or his business capacity has outgrown his home city, and he hopes to find more opportunity in the capital, to make more money.' This quotation reveals something of the weakness of Jefferson's so-called 'law'. In fact, it is no law at all. Jefferson provides us with little more than speculation about a supposed process of urban growth which he fails to substantiate with firm evidence or statistical analysis.

A more scientific explanation for variations in primacy levels has been offered by **A. Linsky** who examined the nations of the world with the highest levels of urban primacy. He demonstrated that many countries with high primacy have the following characteristics: small territorial extent, relatively high population density, high rates of population growth, low per capita incomes, reliance on agricultural exports, and former colonial status. Many of these attributes are, of course, typical of developing nations. Conversely, Linsky showed that many nations with low primacy display characteristics of developed nations, such as slow rates of population growth, non-agricultural economies, higher per capita incomes, and so on. The implication of his findings is that a high level of urban primacy tends to be associated with developing nations whereas a low level of primacy is more typical of developed nations. In other

Jefferson's 'Law of the Primate City' is reviewed in this paragraph. You are unlikely to be able to produce direct quotations as here, but you should at least be able to summarise Jefferson's ideas.

Later work by Linsky is summarised in this paragraph. The variables which Linsky correlated with high and low primacy are listed. A key point here is the contrast in primacy ratios between developed and developing nations. Stemming from that, a time dimension is introduced into the discussion. An ability to relate urban primacy to the stage reached in a nation's economic development would distinguish the best answers to the question.

By way of a conclusion, the ideas of Jefferson and Linsky are contrasted in the final paragraph.

words, urban primacy is essentially a product of the stage reached in the economic development of a nation.

It is evident that the views of Jefferson and Linsky are contradictory. Jefferson suggests that, as a result of multiplier effects and the process of cumulative causation, urban primacy will increase over time. The largest city will become ever larger and draw further away from the second city in size and importance. On the other hand, Linsky suggests that industrialisation and urbanisation will cause cities other than the primate city to grow in size and importance, thus reducing the gap between the primate and lower order cities. That is to say, urban primacy will decrease over time. In the light of the contradiction, further research on the causes of variations in urban primacy would seem to be warranted.

General comments

A word of warning — this whole area of work dealing with the relationships between settlements in terms of their size, spacing and function is regularly tested by means of data-response questions. There are many related graphs and diagrams which lend themselves perfectly to that type of question. You might be given an actual rank-size plot for a particular country and be asked to explain it, or a series of rank-size graphs which you have to compare. You might be presented with a section of the Christaller network and be asked to analyse it, or different versions of the Christaller network which you are asked to explain.

Related questions

1   Comment on the view that 'the Rank-size Rule is little more than a statement of the obvious decorated with a little mathematics'.

2   Explain why developing nations tend to be characterised by high levels of urban primacy.

3   Is there any underlying logic or rationale in the location and spacing of settlements in the landscape?

Question 31

Write a critical evaluation of the various methods
which may be employed to delimit urban fields.

This is a relatively straightforward question with no obvious pitfalls or traps. Provided that
you have carefully prepared and revised this topic it should present few problems. The
key to success is careful essay planning. In general terms there are two contrasting
approaches to the problem of delimiting urban fields. Firstly, there are various empirical
techniques which involve measuring and mapping what is actually going on in reality. What
is the catchment area of a particular shopping centre, school or hospital? Secondly, there is
a theoretical, mathematical approach. This involves arguments and deductions about what
might be expected to happen if certain conditions are fulfilled.

In planning your answer, it is important to allocate roughly equal length and weight to the
two approaches. In this sample answer, each approach has been given three paragraphs.
Both sections of the answer include description and evaluation, focusing on the strengths
and weaknesses of the methodology. It goes without saying that the main body of the essay
is prefaced by an introduction (definitions of terms) and followed by a conclusion (overall
evaluation and summary). This is a simple, straightforward, balanced, effective essay plan.

Answer

Guidance notes

The term 'urban field' is used to describe the area surrounding
a town or city which is linked economically and socially to the
central settlement. Urban fields are also designated by a variety
of other terms, including catchment area, sphere of influence,
tributary area, umland, city region and hinterland. Geographers
have devoted considerable attention to the problems of delimiting urban fields. Early studies of urban field analysis published
in the 1930s indicate the long continuing interest in this aspect
of urban geography. Essentially, two approaches may be identified. First, there are **empirical methods** of study which attempt
to plot the actual social and economic links which exist between
any city and its surrounding regions. Secondly, there are various
theoretical methods which attempt to show what links ought

The term 'urban field', the subject
of the question, is defined in the
introduction. The two contrasting
approaches to its study are also
established right at the end of the
introduction. In that way a link is
made with the paragraph which
follows. Where possible, try to
make connections between
paragraphs.

Description and evaluation of the first approach starts here, and is dealt with in this and the following two paragraphs. If you have studied the urban field of a particular town, then mention it in this section of the answer. Examiners will award marks for evidence of relevant local studies and fieldwork.

to exist or might be expected to exist between city and region, given certain conditions, such as size of the central city and distance from competing urban centres. These two approaches may be considered in turn.

The **empirical approach** to urban field delimitation involves the selection of a number of indices which reflect something of the range of functions of the town in question. Indicators of the town's role as a centre of employment, retailing, marketing, entertainment and administration might be included in a typical package of measures that could be used for the purpose of delimiting its urban field. Each of the selected indices should yield data which can be reduced to a single linear boundary marking the limit of the town's influence over the surrounding area. Measures which have been used by geographers for this purpose include the catchment area of secondary schools, colleges and general hospitals, the delivery areas of large retail stores, the place of residence of workers in city factories and offices, newspaper circulation areas, and many others.

Unfortunately, the city-centred approach is not without its **problems**. The choice of indices is completely subjective, and tests have shown that different measures produce significantly different urban field boundaries. Furthermore, the results for even one indicator can vary according to choice of unit. For example, the delivery areas for different retail stores vary according to the type of goods sold and company policy; similarly, the catchment areas of different factories vary according to the relative attraction of working conditions, wage-rates and other considerations. A more obvious problem is that the boundaries produced by the various indices never coincide exactly. The end result of this type of exercise is a series of **overlapping boundaries** which show little more than the approximate limit of a town's sphere of influence. These diverse boundaries can, of course, be reduced to a single average boundary position, but that too is neither realistic nor satisfactory.

Underlying these difficulties is the fact that the margin of any urban field rarely forms a linear boundary, except in those special circumstances where it is terminated by a state boundary, shoreline or similar barrier. In reality, the socio-economic influence of any town or city gradually diminishes outwards from the urban core. In other words, the boundary is **zonal** rather than linear. Areas lying between two or more urban centres usually lie within overlapping spheres of influence. This fact suggests another approach to the problem of delimitation. As well as adopting the urban-centred techniques described above, it is also possible to reverse the approach by direct attention to the rural inhabitants themselves and analysing their patterns of movement and choices of towns for different goods and services. This might involve a study of rural bus services and passenger flows to adjacent towns, or might take into account the number of railway season-tickets or day-return tickets issued for travel to nearby towns. Data can also be derived from questionnaire surveys among the rural inhabitants about their choice of towns for work, shopping and entertainment. Working in this way, H.E. Bracey was able to construct detailed maps showing what he termed the **intensive, extensive and fringe** areas of the urban fields of Weston-super-Mare and Bridgwater in Somerset.

Various quantitative techniques have also been applied to the problem of urban field delimitation in an attempt to eliminate the subjectivity and lack of precision involved in the various empirical methods described above. These mathematical techniques are derived from the gravity model which is widely used to study interaction between urban centres. For example, it is possible to calculate the position of a **breaking-point** between two towns. This is the point which theoretically divides the people who will travel to one town for goods and services from those who will travel to the other. Clearly, if a series of breaking points are calculated between a given town and all the surrounding towns of the same functional importance, then these points could be connected to produce a theoretical urban field for the town in question. The position of each breaking point (x) can be calculated using the following formula, in which Pi and Pj are the populations of the two towns; dij is the distance between them, and djx is the distance of the breaking point from the smaller town, j.

$$djx = \frac{dij}{1 + \sqrt{\dfrac{Pi}{Pj}}}$$

Figure 1 Position of the breaking-point between two towns, i and j

In a similar way, W.J. Reilly's **Law of Retail Trade Gravitation**, also a derivation of the basic gravity model formula, can be used to predict the proportion of retail trade which two towns will derive from a settlement lying between them. Again, this is relevant to the theoretical delimitation of urban fields. If a

This is an early study of urban fields. By mentioning such work you are demonstrating to the examiner that you have done some background reading on this topic.

Description and evaluation of the theoretical approach starts here. It involves discussion of so-called Breaking-point Theory and the Law of Retail Trade Gravitation, both derived from the basic gravity model.

There is no expectation that you should be able to reproduce this formula from memory in the exam. That will be a feature of only the very best answers. However, you should be able to demonstrate an understanding of the principles and concepts implicit in Breaking-point Theory, and be able to discuss it in general terms.

village is found to patronise the two towns equally, then it must be located exactly on the breaking-point between them. If, on the other hand, the greater part of its retailing takes place in one town rather than the other, then clearly it lies within the catchment of that particular town.

Both the breaking-point formula and the Law of Retail Trade Gravitation suffer from a number of limitations. They are based on various **assumptions** which cannot be justified in reality. They assume, for example, that the attraction of a town or city is determined simply by its population size. The bigger the town, the stronger its attraction. They assume too that people will organise their shopping expeditions in a rational, logical manner, selecting the town which is nearest in terms of time or distance. None of this is necessarily the case. Small towns with high quality shops many be more attractive than large industrial towns with poor quality, deteriorated shopping facilities. In any case, people do not necessarily organise their activities in the most rational or economic way. Rural populations may have incomplete or incorrect information about urban services, and many perceive and evaluate travel distances in a distorted manner. For example, a study of retailing in the San Francisco Bay Area revealed that customers frequently over-estimated the distance to what they regarded as unattractive shopping centres, and under-estimated the distance to high quality, prestigious shopping areas. It was concluded that 'neat, often circular, market areas drawn on a map may be a very poor representation of geographic purchasing patterns dependent on highly variable human behaviour'.

Despite the large number of methods available for the delimitation of urban fields, none are wholly satisfactory. Empirical methods tend to be subjective and lack the precision expected of modern geographical studies. On the other hand, the abstract, mathematical methods derived from the gravity model are based on assumptions about human behaviour and decision-making which cannot be justified in reality. It might be argued that a combination of the inductive and deductive approaches is needed to achieve the best possible result to what is clearly a difficult problem.

The conclusion is quite brief and predictable. It simply attempts to summarise and draw together some of the findings in the main body of the essay.

General Comments

This is the type of question which can be best answered if you have actually attempted to use the techniques involved. It is possible that you may have used the empirical methods on a field-course or in the context of a personal enquiry or project, or maybe attempted to use the mathematical techniques in a class exercise. Whenever possible, always work personal experiences of that kind into your answers.

Related questions

1 Assess the relative merits of empirical and theoretical techniques employed in the delimitation of urban fields.

2 Identify and comment on the various factors which influence the size and shape of urban fields.

3 What factors would have to be taken into account in order to determine the optimum location for a large out-of-town shopping centre?

Define the term 'rural–urban fringe'. Identify and describe its main physical and social characteristics.

Tackling the question

This is a very traditional type of question. It is not broken up into numbered sections, and no mark allocations are indicated for the various parts of the question. Thus, the answer should be written as a formal essay, with ideas and information presented in well-structured paragraphs which are arranged in a clear logical sequence.

The question includes three 'task-words': define, identify and describe. These should be considered carefully when planning your answer. In the sample answer, the first paragraph addresses the first of these tasks and defines the term rural–urban fringe. Definitions can usually be kept quite short and concise. In this case the definition also doubles as the introduction to the essay. Next, an attempt is made to identify and describe the physical characteristics of the fringe belt. This is followed by the identification and description of the social characteristics of the rural–urban fringe. The final paragraph seeks to remind the reader that the rural–urban fringe is a non-static, contantly evolving feature. It also serves as the conclusion to the essay.

Answer

The question asks for a definition. This paragraph provides a composite definition, drawing on several different views and interpretations of the rural–urban fringe.

Towns do not exist in isolation. They draw in workers, shoppers and visitors from their surrounding area, and, conversely distribute goods and services to areas beyond their boundaries. This sphere of social and economic interaction between town and country is known as the urban field of any town. The term 'rural–urban fringe', or 'rurban fringe' as it is sometimes known, is used to refer to the areas immediately beyond the municipal boundary of any town, but still firmly within the influence of the town in question. In other words, the rural–urban fringe may be thought of as the innermost zone of the urban field. The rural–urban fringe is a **zone of transition** in which rural and urban characteristics co-exist in uneasy and often conflicting juxtaposition. It has frequently been pointed out that it is impossible to draw a satisfactory boundary between rural and urban areas. For example, as early as 1953, A.E. Smailes noted that 'there is no longer either socially or physically a simple clear-cut dichotomy of town and country: rather, it is an urban-rural continuum.... There is no definite point where rural ends and urban begins.' The rural–urban fringe is simply part of the continuum between town and country. Not surprisingly, therefore, it has also been described as 'a geographical no-man's land' (R.G. Golledge), not yet wholly urbanised, but at the same time no longer essentially rural. These general characteristics are summarised in the *Dictionary of Human Geography* (1989) which defines the rural–urban fringe as 'a transitory zone of mixed rural and urban land uses at the edge of large cities'. The typical width of this zone has been variously described as ranging between about 2 km (Countryside Commission) and 10 km (R. Munton and C. Harrison).

Consideration of the **physical characteristics** of the rural–urban fringe is mainly concerned with the typical **land use** features of this zone immediately beyond the contiguous built-up area of large cities. As mentioned above, it contains both urban and rural characteristics. Many of the **urban features** are those which service the city but are either too **space-consuming** or **noxious** (creating noise, dust, fumes, etc.) to be located within the actual built-up area of the city. Typically, such land uses include airports, railway marshalling yards, water works, sewage works, junkyards, refuse dumps, power stations, sand and gravel pits and other mineral workings, sports grounds, golf courses, etc. The rural–urban fringe also contains **residential areas**, representing different stages in the irregular outward growth of the city into adjacent greenfield sites. Typically, it also contains much **derelict land**. In many cases this is a result of developers and speculators buying up plots to create 'banks' of land which are simply held for re-selling or development at some future date when land values have risen in anticipation of continued urban expansion. In the meantime, such areas are often poorly maintained and contribute to the general air of neglect and dereliction which is typical of the approaches into most large cities. Patterns of land use such as this have been described and analysed around many cities; for example R.G. Golledge's work on the fringe zone of Sydney, Australia, and J. Giggs' analysis of fringe expansion and suburbanisation around Nottingham.

The rural–urban fringe also contains some residual **rural features** which struggle for survival in the face of the relentless encroachment of the adjacent city. Usually, some agricultural activity still takes place, often under the most difficult conditions. Farms are generally small, and produce crops and livestock for the adjacent urban market. Numerous studies have emphasised the difficulties under which these smallholders operate. For example, a survey of 100 **farms** in the vicinity of Slough to the

The section on physical characteristics is mainly about land use. This paragraph describes features resulting from urban encroachment. The following paragraph describes residual rural features.

Clear evidence of reading on this topic will earn marks.

Useful reference to a relevant case study.

This paragraph is about land use conflicts and attempts at planning in the rural–urban fringe.

This and the following paragraph demonstrate an awareness of the work of two important contributors to the study of urban fringe belts: A. Coleman (on land use) and R.E. Pahl (on social characteristics).

The section on social characteristics is mainly about the social changes which have taken place in fringe belt towns and villages as a result of the growth of commuting.

west of London revealed problems of damage to crops, fences, hedges, gates and equipment, **theft** of crops and machinery, dumping of rubbish in fields and hedgerows, **trespass** and worrying of livestock by dogs, and so on. Clearly, the juxtaposition of farmland and housing estates is a potential source of conflict and expense for farmers and smallholders seeking to make a living in that situation.

The incompatible juxtaposition of farming and housing described above is just one of many land use conflicts found in the rural–urban fringe. As a result of these conflicts, planners have attempted to impose controls on development in such areas. These aim to progressively reduce, and ultimately eliminate, the conflicts stemming from incompatible land uses. In its most extreme manifestations, planning control has taken the form of **green belts** (e.g. the London Green belt) within which most planning applications for new development are rejected. Other planning devices include **zoning policies, land use restrictions, conservation areas,** etc. However, an examination of land use patterns around most large cities suggests that these policies have had only a limited effect. Alice Coleman, for example, has described rural–urban fringe areas in the UK as 'a failure of planning'.

The **social characteristics** of the rural–urban fringe also stem from its transitional location between town and country. Based on a study of the Hertfordshire section of London's fringe belt, R.E. Pahl has suggested that it contains two types of occupier; first, true, indigenous, mainly working-class, **rural residents**, and secondly, newly arrived, mainly middle-class **urbanised residents** still retaining strong links with the city. The two groups have different lifestyles and different types of occupations, and tend to live socially and physically segregated lives in so-called '**metropolitan villages**' within the fringe zone. The newcomers commute to work in the city and use it regularly for shopping and entertainment, while the long-term, indigenous residents generally work and shop locally. Pahl notes that, 'a new population is invading local communities, bringing in urban values and class consciousness'. Thus, according to this view, the rural–urban fringe is not only characterised by a distinctive pattern of land use, but also by an invasion of mobile, middle-class families orientated towards the city and still dominated by urban lifestyles.

Social changes in turn produce physical changes in the areas most affected. Increased levels of commuting produces congestion on narrow rural roads quite unsuited for heavy volumes of traffic. Public transport systems are loaded to breaking point at rush-hour times, and then stand idle for much of the rest of the day. In the actual commuter-villages changes take place which reflect the tastes and needs of the urbanised newcomers; antique shops, picture galleries, health-food shops and delicatessens, wine-bars and restaurants replace traditional village retail outlets. In these ways the former rural way of life becomes progressively submerged beneath an advancing tide of suburbanisation. A recent article on 'The Commuter Effect' asked the question, 'Are there any true villages left in Hampshire?...If the answer appears to be a reverberating silence, this is because the people who could give it are presently not at home. They have Chubb-locked their dream cottage, risen even earlier than their neighbour to berth the Saab at Basingstoke, and are hurtling to Waterloo through the last little bits of green that hold the homes apart in Surrey.' (*The Times*, 15 August 1989)

> This quotation is not essential but gives 'colour' to the answer. It also shows that useful geographical material can be found in the quality newspapers. Clip and file relevant newspaper articles with your notes.

Finally, discussion of the rural–urban fringe requires some reference to a time dimension. Both its physical and social characteristics are determined by the stage reached in its development. At an early stage, the fringe zone may be dominated by untouched villages and unspoilt countryside, but as the city expands outwards, the mixture of rural and urban characteristics becomes progressively dominated by urban elements. Eventually, in the final stage of development, former fringe zones become fully incorporated into the urban fabric. Several writers have shown how features of former fringe belts even continue to influence the morphology of urban areas long after their incorporation into it. Simultaneously with the process of assimilation, the rural–urban fringe moves outwards, away from the city, so that a whole new cycle of invasion by urban land uses and urban residents begins again. Around Britain's largest towns and cities, this process has continued relentlessly for more than a hundred years. The results have generally been destructive and detrimental.

General comments

The sample answer has a missing ingredient. It contains no evidence of personal observation; no reference to rural–urban fringe areas known to the writer; no case-study material other than that derived from books and journals. The essay contains references to various locations — Sydney, Nottingham, Slough, Hertfordshire, Basingstoke, etc. — but all of them are 'second-hand', extracted from published sources. They are certainly better than nothing, and will attract marks from the examiner; but how much better the essay would have been if it had included evidence of personal observation.

Related questions

1 To what extent is it appropriate to describe the rural–urban fringe around large British cities as 'a failure of planning'?

2 Make a critical evaluation of the effectiveness of green-belt policies in the UK.

3 With reference to actual areas, examine the particular problems faced by farmers and smallholders operating in urban fringe locations.

Question 33

What do you consider to be the main changes taking place in the traditional English village?

Tackling the question

This is a very wide question, posed in very general terms. Faced with such a question in the examination, you need to produce an essay plan which makes the question more focused. Try to break the question down into specific themes. In that way it becomes much easier to handle. The question asks about 'changes' taking place in traditional villages. What categories of change can you identify? Make a list of categories; for example, economic, physical (structural), demographic, social, etc. Each one could constitute a paragraph in your answer. What is the time-scale for the discussion? The wording of the question gives a clue. It refers to changes 'taking place' (present tense). Presumably, therefore, the examiner requires you to place the emphasis on contemporary or recent changes. The question asks about changes taking place in the 'traditional' English village, not all villages. Again, this gives you another theme for discussion.

Answer

Almost everyone has an **image** of the traditional English village. For the town-dweller, removed from country life, that image is based more on nostalgia than on reality. The idealised picture probably includes thatched cottages of mellow brick or stone arranged around a village green. The quintessential village would probably be thought of as having an ancient church, a traditional pub and a small village store supplying basic needs. It would house a largely self-sufficient community, isolated from urban influences, with its economic life firmly based on agriculture and associated craft industries. In reality, many traditional English villages have changed beyond recognition during the present century. Villages are no longer necessarily dependent on the land. Thus, there are now villages which live on tourism, villages which house mostly commuters or weekenders, even villages dominated by light industry. Another trend is for people to live in villages, working from home by linking up with their city employers through computers. Increasingly, there is less and less accordance between image and reality.

Guidance notes

What is meant by a 'traditional English village'? Consideration of this question provides an appropriate introduction to the essay. The closing sentence of the paragraph 'flags' the main themes which follow.

Main categories of change are now identified and discussed paragraph by paragraph. This and the following paragraph deal with economic and social changes. Notice how the final sentence of paragraph three provides a link with paragraph four, which discusses rural depopulation and its effects.

Before considering the nature of these changes in detail, it may be useful to examine the **economic and social background** which helps to explain them. A key factor has been the huge reduction in the agricultural labour force resulting from mechanisation. This has radically changed the rural occupation structure, which was an essential aspect of the traditional village community. Not only has the number of farm-workers in Britain declined from almost 2 million in 1861 to 150,000 at the present time, but associated rural trades have also declined. Blacksmiths, wheelwrights, saddle-makers and thatchers have all experienced a sharp decline in the demand for their services. Indeed, most have now completely disappeared from village life. Corn-grinding has moved from the villages to large modern mills in the towns. Small-scale rural manufacturing has also been unable to compete with large-scale urban industry. Furniture workshops have virtually disappeared from the Chiltern villages, paper-mills from Devon valleys and small textile-mills from East Anglia.

Not only has rural employment been lost, but living standards in many rural areas have remained depressingly low. Housing conditions in many villages lag far behind those of the towns in respect of piped water-supply, gas, electricity and mains drainage. Overcrowding is common in many homes with several generations of a farming family often occupying a small tied cottage or house. Nor are improvements easy in an occupation which has long paid wages substantially lower than those in the secondary and tertiary sectors. For many, the city is seen as the only means of escape from an environment which offers few opportunities and little prospect for personal advancement. Radio and television have made many villagers more aware of alternatives. Urban attractions are thought to include better shopping facilities, better housing, greater opportunities for educational advancement, and a wider range of entertainment and recreational facilities. The fact that many of these attractions are imagined rather than real is irrelevant. A fourfold increase in private car ownership in the last 30 years has also had the effect of making towns more accessible and breaking down rural isolation.

One response to the socio-economic changes outlined above has been a growing movement of population away from many rural areas. **Rural depopulation** may be seen as a reaction to the conditions of high unemployment, low wages, poor housing and limited amenities. Many of those who move away are young adults, which has the effect of causing an ageing of population and a lowering of birth rate which, in turn, also contributes to the long-term process of depopulation. Furthermore, as village populations fall below critical threshold levels, even basic services start to be reduced. The village school may close, bus services may be reduced, and other essential services may be transferred to nearby towns. As a consequence, more jobs are lost, the village becomes even less attractive, and depopulation accelerates. The process is a cumulative one. However, the movement of population is not one-way. At the same time as the rural population is moving away, an influx of newcomers into the village can often be noted. These new arrivals are mostly middle-class families moving from the city in search of larger, cheaper homes in attractive rural surroundings. Some are elderly couples moving to the country on retirement. Thus, by the twin processes of flow and counter-flow, the social structure of the village becomes radically changed.

The process of **urbanisation** may take many forms. One obvious manifestation is the growth of **commuter villages** in the rural areas adjacent to large towns and cities. In these villages, relatively wealthy upper- and middle-class families, although resident in the village, still retain strong links with the city for work, shopping, entertainment and social contacts. In this way, the population of such villages becomes sharply polarised into affluent, middle-class newcomers retaining urban links, and a residue of working-class, long-term residents who are still strongly village-orientated.

Another form of urbanisation is the proliferation of **second homes** in many villages. Most are found within a reasonable driving distance from large cities and are used for weekend or holiday visits. Favoured areas in Britain include North Norfolk and Suffolk, North and Central Wales, Devon and Cornwall and the New Forest area of Hampshire. Wide differences of opinion are held about the social and economic consequences of the growing movement towards second-home ownership. Significantly, one book on the subject by J.T. Coppock is entitled *Second Homes. Curse or Blessing?* Some regard the process as a useful economic stimulus in declining villages, creating increased demand for local goods and services. Others view the process with alarm, arguing that it contributes to the breakdown of traditional rural society and deprives local residents of homes which stand empty for most of the year.

Yet another form of urbanisation of villages relates to the increasing use of the countryside by town-dwellers for **leisure and recreation activities**. Tourism is now the most rapidly growing form of urban encroachment on the countryside. Again, there are advantages and disadvantages. Hotels and boarding houses enjoy a busy trade, and village shops and other services benefit from increased patronage. The price for all of this is traffic congestion in narrow country lanes, litter and pollution near picnic areas and beauty spots, and conflict between the interests of farmers and visitors.

Not only is the demographic and social structure of the traditional English village changing as a result of the simultaneous

Another linking section here. The influx of newcomers from the city is mentioned briefly, and then the theme is picked up and developed in the next three paragraphs which discuss different aspects of urbanisation.

Good detail; reference to some popular locations for second homes and mention of an important book on the subject.

Finally, the impacts of economic, social and demographic change are discussed. Destruction of the traditional appearance and character of villages provides both a synthesis and a conclusion for the answer.

processes of rural depopulation and urbanisation, but the morphology (or physical structure) of the village is changing too, as it responds to the tastes and lifestyles of the newcomers. Suburban-style housing estates, strangely out-of-keeping with traditional rural domestic buildings, have been grafted onto many villages with disastrous results. Patterns of local retailing have been transformed in many commuter villages. Former grocery shops and hardware stores have been replaced by health-food stores, delicatessens, antique shops and art galleries, all reflecting the middle-class urban tastes of the newcomers to the village. The overall effect of these socio-economic changes is to blur the distinction between town and country. Certainly, villages no longer house isolated, independent populations which they once did. The true character of the traditional English village has been largely replaced by a 'cosmetic rurality' imposed upon it by a newly-arrived population. The traditional English village based upon the local agricultural economy may have been less than idyllic for those who actually lived and worked there. Nevertheless, its demise is observed with concern and sadness by those who care for the English rural heritage.

General comments

Questions on current and recent changes in rural areas in Britain appear quite frequently in the A-level examination. Some are concerned with the countryside in general — land use changes, the impacts of new farming techniques, the growing use of the countryside for leisure and recreation, and the need for careful planning and management of countryside areas. Other questions, as here, focus specifically on rural settlements, and are largely concerned with the effects of counter-urbanisation on small towns and villages.

Related questions

1   Many rural areas in Britain suffer from a variety of social and economic problems. Identify these problems, and examine the planning strategies which have been devised to deal with them.

2   Examine the impacts of tourism in any one named rural area.

3   'Second homes. Curse or blessing?' Elaborate on the costs and benefits of the growth of second homes in many rural areas of Britain.

Question 34

Describe and comment on the use of the nearest-neighbour statistic in the analysis of rural settlement patterns.

Tackling the question

This question asks you to describe and comment on the application of a particular technique employed in the statistical analysis of spatial or geographical patterns; namely, the technique of nearest-neighbour analysis. Obviously, if the examiners decide to test your understanding of this technique, they have two options. Firstly, they could present you with some sort of applied test, providing you with an actual distribution pattern which you then have to analyse using the nearest-neighbour statistic. Alternatively, they could ask you simply to describe and appraise the technique. This question is of the latter type. Obviously, if you have used the technique in class or on a field-course, you will be in a good position to answer the question, relating it to your own experience. If you have only read about but never actually used the technique, then the question is probably best left alone.

Answer

As well as considering the distribution of towns and cities, Christaller's central place theory also includes reference to the spacing of villages, hamlets, and other low-order settlements in the landscape. According to Christaller, small clusters of dwellings or hamlets would be more or less self-sufficient at the time of establishment and would require similar amounts of land to support their populations. According to Christaller's calculations, this would produce an even distribution of hamlets, each about 4 km from its neighbour. Similarly, trading hamlets or villages would assume an even distribution at a distance of about 7 km from each other. However, since the isotropic conditions of the Christaller model are never fulfilled, this theoretical pattern provides no more than a starting point in the analysis of rural settlement patterns. In reality, settlement spacing is far more complex than central place theory would suggest. Irregularities and distortions of the theoretical model are caused by the unique local circumstances of relief, drainage, climate and soils, and the particular historical evolution of any area.

Guidance notes

The context for the question is the spacing of small towns and villages in a rural setting. Classic work on settlement spacing was carried out by Christaller (1933), so it seems appropriate to mention his model as an introduction to the topic.

The need for a precise statistical measure is discussed in this paragraph.

This is one of a relatively small number of mathematical formulae which you should commit to memory as part of your preparation for the exam, although in data-response questions the formula is usually provided.

This paragraph identifies the range of possible results for the test, and then examines how those results may be interpreted.

Given this complexity, a basic problem facing the geographer is that of finding a 'language' which is capable of describing particular settlement patterns and comparing one with another. **Descriptive terms**, such as 'dispersed' and 'nucleated' or 'evenly spaced' and 'clustered', lack precision. Using that kind of vague descriptive terminology, it is difficult to know whether villages in one region are more clustered than those in another. In fact, precise comparisons are impossible. Early attempts to advance the analysis of rural settlement patterns beyond the simple descriptive terms 'dispersed' and 'nucleated' involved the formulation of various **coefficients of nucleation and dispersion**. These attempted to measure the extent to which rural population was concentrated in villages, as opposed to being scattered throughout the countryside in farms and cottages outside the villages. What was also needed was an index or measure to express the actual patterns of spacing of the village settlements themselves. This need has been met by the application of the technique of nearest-neighbour analysis to the study of rural settlement spacing.

Nearest-neighbour analysis, which was first devised by botanists to describe plant distributions, involves the calculation of a **nearest-neighbour index** (R_n) by means of the following formula:

$$R_n = 2d \sqrt{\frac{n}{A}}$$

in which 'A' is the size of the study area (km^2), 'd' is the mean distance between the nearest villages (km), and 'n' is the number of villages in the study area. In order to obtain the 'd' value, it is necessary to consider each village in turn. Its nearest-neighbour is identified, and the distance between that pair of villages is measured. 'd' is the mean of those distances.

In theory, values for R_n will lie within the range from zero to 2.15. Zero would signify **total concentration**, whereby in theory all villages occupy the same location, while a value of 2.15 would signify perfectly **even spacing**, with each village absolutely equi-distant from its neighbours. In reality, neither of these extreme values is ever obtained. A nearest-neighbour index of 1.0 indicates **random spacing**, with no tendency towards either clustering or even spacing. This should not be taken to mean that the location of the various villages is a product of chance. The advantage of the nearest-neighbour index is that it provides an exact quantitative measure of spacing. It enables patterns of rural settlement to be compared with a degree of precision which would not be possible in general descriptive terms. For example, villages in Region A may give an index of 0.65; villages in Region B may give an index of 0.59. This reveals that the spacing of villages in Region B is slightly more clustered than in Region A.

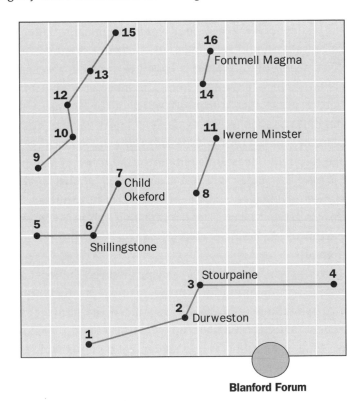

Note: The location of villages has been plotted from the Ordnance Survey map of the area. Each square on the grid represents 1 km². Nearest-neighbours are indicated by linking lines. Thus, the nearest-neighbour of Village 3 is Village 2; the nearest-neighbour of Village 4 is Village 3, and so on.

Figure 1   Distribution of villages in the area north of Blanford Forum in Dorset

This answer uses an actual settlement pattern derived from an Ordnance Survey map. In an examination you could easily make up a hypothetical example to demonstrate how the technique works. In the same way, you should be able to construct your own diagram similar to Figure 2 (below).

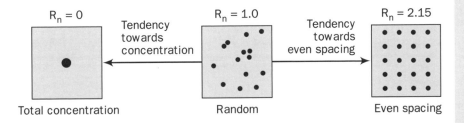

Figure 2   A continuum of spacing from concentration (clustering) to even spacing

In practice, the use of the nearest-neighbour index is not quite as simple as it might first appear. A number of **problems** involved in its use should be noted. The first concerns the selection of settlements. Should small hamlets be included? If not, how is a distinction to be drawn between hamlet and village? Another problem relates to the location of the point used for measurement. It is not always easy to locate a geographic centre in long straggling 'street villages' or in loosely-structured villages lacking a clearly defined centre. Another question is

This paragraph identifies some of the problems involved in applying the technique, and the following paragraph mentions limitations of possible results.

whether or not villages just beyond the study area should be included. In Figure 1, the nearest-neighbour to Village 4 is Village 3. But, what if another village lay just to the east of Village 4, just outside the study area? That would greatly reduce the 'd' value for Village 4, and would significantly affect the overall result. Should it be taken into account or ignored?

Even when these problems have been solved, the nearest-neighbour index still suffers from a number of **limitations**. In particular, it can give a misleading result for certain types of spatial pattern, such as, for example, a linear pattern produced by pairs of villages on opposite sides of a river. Because each village forms the nearest-neighbour of the other village in the pair, a very low index will result, suggesting almost total concentration of villages, which, of course, is not the case. The index also tends to cancel out contrasting sub-patterns, which may exist in an area, to give an exaggerated impression of randomness.

Nevertheless, despite the problems involved in its construction and certain limitations in its results, the technique of nearest-neighbour analysis has advanced the study of rural settlement patterns from mere subjective description. It is particularly good in revealing village settlement patterns which have a marked tendency towards clustering or even-spacing. It goes without saying that one should be very cautious in inferring causes or processes from particular point patterns. 'Like all statistical methods, it [the nearest-neighbour index] should be applied with caution and common sense. The value of the interpretation of the results depends on the judgement and skill of the investigator.' (R. Hammond and P.S. McCullagh)

The conclusion takes the form of an evaluation of the merits and defects of the nearest-neighbour statistic. It finishes with a quotation. A nice flourish, but one which you are unlikely to be able to match in an examination.

General comments

This is rather like Question 20 which asks about the use of the Lorenz Curve in population analysis. This question is concerned with the application of a particular statistical technique to the analysis of rural settlement patterns. In both cases the technique is quite easy to use in practice, but quite difficult to describe in words. You need to discuss the methodology, stage by stage, keeping your account as clear and concise as possible. You may find it helps to relate your account to an actual example or even a hypothetical example. Also bear in mind that this particular technique is more likely to be tested with a data-response question.

Related questions

1   According to Christaller, under idealised conditions, villages will tend to be evenly spaced in the landscape. What are those idealised conditions, and how do 'real-world' conditions cause distortions and modifications to Christaller's model?

2   Describe how the nearest-neighbour statistic might be employed to analyse the distribution of banks in a large city centre.

3   Can the nearest-neighbour statistic reveal anything about rural settlement spacing that is not immediately evident from simple map analysis?

Question 35

(a) Discuss the circumstances which have produced spatial concentrations of elderly population.

(b) Comment on the social and economic problems caused by such concentrations.

Tackling the question

This is a two-part question with clearly designated sections. No mark allocations are indicated for the two parts, so it should be assumed that they carry equal weight. Thus, in the sample answer, the two sections are of similar length and contain roughly similar amounts of information and detail. The two opening paragraphs serve as an introduction to both answers. The first paragraph establishes the context for the two answers, and the second defines the term 'elderly population' and suggests a useful subdivision of this age cohort.

Section (a) employs a commonly-used and effective device which is to look at distribution patterns at different scales — national, regional and local. Concentrations of elderly produced by retirement migration are contrasted with concentrations of elderly 'trapped' in inner city districts. Section (b) attempts to give a balanced presentation of both the positive and negative consequences of concentrations of elderly population.

Answer

The term '**social gerontology**' is used to describe the field of study concerned with the social, economic and demographic conditions of the elderly, as well as government policy and provision for the elderly. Until recently, the field of social gerontology had been largely neglected by geographers, despite its potential for spatial analysis. However, with the modern focus of social geography on social problems, a number of geographers have turned their attention to the study and analysis of elderly population. The range of issues which has attracted the attention of geographers is usefully summarised in the collection of essays edited by A.M. Warnes *Geographical Perspectives on the Elderly*. These include contributions on the process of demographic ageing, the distribution of elderly population, the behaviour and activity patterns of the elderly, and the provision and accessibility of welfare and specialist health services for the elderly.

For purposes of study, it is normal to define elderly population as those above the age of retirement. In the UK these include females above the age of 60 years and males above the age of 65 years. A distinction is often drawn between '**elderly**' and '**very elderly**' population; the former aged 60 or 65 to 75 years, and the latter more than 75 years of age. As a group, the elderly have a number of distinguishing features; namely, lower incomes than the economically active population, increasing dependence on welfare services, declining physical capabilities and increasing dependence on relatives, friends and social services. As a group, the elderly are also characterised by a predominance of females.

(a) The **spatial distribution** of elderly population may be considered at different scales. On a **world scale**, it is a fact that the developed nations contain a greater proportion of elderly population than the developing nations. The developed nations enjoy lower mortality rates and have a longer expectation of life, so that a greater proportion of the population survives into old age. At a **regional scale**, it can be observed that in many countries there are regional variations in the proportion of elderly population. The point may be illustrated by reference to England and Wales.

Between 1921 and 1991 the total population of England and Wales rose from 37.9 million to 50.9 million (+34.3%) while the number of elderly people rose from 3.0 million to 9.4 million (+213.3.0%). While the overall population growth was concentrated in South-East England, the growth of elderly population was concentrated in very different regions — mainly peripheral coastal areas such as Devon, Cornwall, Somerset, Dorset, Kent, Sussex, Norfolk, Suffolk, Cumbria, Gwynedd and Clwyd. By 1991 several of these counties had over 25% elderly population, compared with an average of 18% for England and Wales as a whole. The spatial concentration of elderly population in these coastal areas and areas of attractive upland scenery can be explained by the process of **retirement migration**. With increased expectation of life, old age has become a stage in life which offers new opportunities for a significant proportion of the population. Freed from the constraint of having to live close to their place of work, many elderly people now have the opportunity to move to a new place of residence which offers various perceived advantages such as attractive coastal or upland scenery, healthier climate, lower house prices, a more tranquil lifestyle, etc. Thus, during 1990 over 130,000 people aged 60 years or more were involved in a change of permanent residence

When responding to questions which require discussion of spatial patterns, it is often useful to consider different geographic scales. In this case, variations at national, regional and local scale are identified.

This answer uses UK examples, but many textbooks contain similar material for other countries. For example, the migration of elderly population to the 'sun-belt' in the USA is well documented.

(almost 30% of all migratory moves). Of these, most moved from large towns and cities to small towns and villages near the seaside or in the country.

Even within the regions mentioned above, there are concentrations of elderly population at **local scale**. That is to say, certain towns and localities are characterised by even higher proportions of old people, with, in some cases, more than 40% of the population above retirement age. For example, Sidmouth (Devon) has 44.3% elderly population, Bexhill (East Sussex) 44.2%, Southwold (Suffolk) 43.8% and Frinton and Walton (Essex) 40.8%. The suggestion has been made that once a particular town or locality starts to attract retired population, there follows a provision of specialist geriatric services (retirement homes, sheltered housing, day centres for the elderly, etc.) so that the process tends to become cumulative.

However, reference to retirement migration should not be allowed to obscure the fact that for a clear majority of elderly people, ageing takes place in the area in which they have spent the greater part of their working life or even the whole of their life. With declining incomes, retirement migration is not even a remote option for most elderly people. Indeed, many old people find themselves 'trapped' in sub-standard housing in inner city districts from which they have little prospect of escape. It frequently happens that the more affluent, economically-active, young adult population moves away from these areas, leaving a **residual population** composed of large numbers of elderly people. Local concentrations of old people can result from this process. Thus, many of the municipal estates in Inner London contain more than 25% retired population, a figure which is significantly higher than that for Greater London as a whole.

> These inner city concentrations of elderly population are frequently under-estimated or ignored. They represent an important form of local concentration.

(b) Clearly, the concentration of large numbers of elderly people in particular areas must have important **social and economic repercussions** on the areas concerned. It is generally assumed that these impacts are largely, or even wholly, negative. That is to say, large numbers of old people are perceived as a burden on the local economy and viewed collectively as a social problem. In support of this **negative view,** it is pointed out that pensioner households have low incomes (about 40% of incomes for households with a working head), and that many old people are impoverished and require various supplementary benefits such as council tax rebates, heating allowances and housing benefits. Furthermore, since they spend less than the working population on food, transport, gas and electricity, their contribution to the local economy is meagre. The point is also made that spatial concentrations of elderly people also require a high level of provision of specialist services such as old people's homes, day-care centres, geriatric wards in hospitals, 'meals-on-wheels' services, etc. It is argued that such services consume a large proportion of local funds, thereby depriving other sectors of the social and welfare services. In the case of seaside resorts with a large retired population, the additional point is sometimes made that the large numbers of elderly people create a 'negative image' for these towns, which has the effect of detracting potential tourists and thereby reducing tourist revenue.

However, there is also a **positive view** of the social and economic impacts of large numbers of elderly people. The argument has been made, for example, that retired people, as non-workers, take nothing from the local area in terms of wages, and simply add to the local economy by spending savings which have been accumulated elsewhere. Some support for this view is provided by an HMSO Report on 'Retirement to the South West'. According to this report, the 140,000 retired people living in Devon and Cornwall contribute £54 million per annum to the regional economy, compared with an income from tourism of £115 million per annum. The same report suggested that the demand for household services by the elderly has the effect of creating employment and boosting the local economy in those parts of South-West England where they are found in large numbers. According to the positive viewpoint, it is also argued that central government funding of Regional Health Service and local government budgets both take into account the numbers of elderly people in the population, and that the effect of a large retired population is to attract funding into an area. It is also suggested that areas with large numbers of elderly people inevitably have relatively small numbers of children, and that the increased costs of geriatric services are therefore offset by the reduced costs of pediatric and educational services.

From these brief summaries of the two opposing viewpoints, it is apparent that the social and economic impacts are not necessarily or wholly negative, as is generally perceived. Impact analysis is clearly complicated, and the costs and benefits involved no doubt vary from one area to another. Much depends on the numbers involved and the costs and quality of local geriatric service provision. With forecasts of a growth in the numbers of elderly people in the UK at least until the end of the century, it is evident that the issues involved will remain important for many years to come.

These counter-arguments are often neglected. In this answer both points of view are given equal weight — one substantial paragraph to each.

The conclusion here is quite brief, but an attempt is made to establish a balanced position, and also to draw attention to the problems of evaluation and measurement.

General comments

The study of elderly population might be a requirement in different parts of your syllabus. For example, age structure is an important aspect of population composition. Retirement migration is an important component of migration studies and also has a role in the process of counter-urbanisation. Additionally, if your syllabus includes sections on social geography or health and welfare, the special needs and service provision for the elderly might be relevant there.

Related questions

1 Write an account of retirement migration in the UK, explaining source and destination areas in terms of 'push–pull' factors.

2 During the present century the proportion of elderly people in Britain has more than doubled. Discuss the circumstances which have produced that change.

3 Discuss the causes and consequences of the concentration of elderly population in many inner city districts.

Question 36

What is meant by the term urban deprivation? Examine the problems involved in identifying and delimiting areas of urban deprivation in British towns and cities.

Tackling the question

This question involves three tasks. Firstly, you are required to define the term 'urban deprivation'. This part of the question is all about terminology and semantics. Secondly, you are required to consider the problems of identifying actual areas of deprivation in British cities. What data are available, and what are their limitations? Thirdly, you are required to discuss the problems of delimitation. How does one draw a boundary line around actual areas of deprivation? The first task is theoretical; the latter two are applied. This is one of those questions where you need to think very carefully about what is needed before rushing into an essay plan.

Answer

Guidance notes

In recent years there has been a growing interest among geographers in the unequal distribution of goods and resources, and the spatial variations in living standards and quality of life. This interest may be related to the emergence of new 'schools' or branches of human geography, variously described as welfare geography, radical geography and Marxist geography. Implicit in much of this recent work is the notion that geographers should move from their traditional neutral stance, whereby they simply mapped and described spatial inequalities of one sort or another, to a more active role in which they should seek to identify causes of social injustice and even attempt to influence social policy. Recent work on deprivation and inequalities, therefore, tends to be of a more applied nature than hitherto.

In the very broadest sense, urban deprivation may be defined as a lack of conditions necessary for the enjoyment of a reasonable standard of living by city-dwellers. The Department of the Environment has suggested that 'deprivation exists when, because of deficiencies of consumption or income in relation to needs, an individual's well-being falls below a level

The introduction simply provides a context for the answer. It attempts to relate the specific theme of deprivation to the broader interest of social geographers in questions of social injustice and inequality.

The first part of the answer starts here. This and the following paragraph are all about definition and terminology. A word of caution — many students use the terms 'poverty' and 'deprivation' as if they were synonymous, which of course they are not.

At this point the answer begins to make reference to actual districts in actual cities. In a sense this forms a bridge between the first and second parts of the question.

generally regarded as a reasonable minimum in Britain today'. Such a definition is, of course, very vague. What is meant by 'a reasonable minimum'? Much depends on the expectations and aspirations of people themselves. A standard of living which might seem positively comfortable to one person, might seem like deprivation to another. A further problem of definition stems from the enormous variety of factors which affect an individual's sense of well-being. These include economic factors such as security of employment, social factors such as housing quality, environmental factors such as the incidence of pollution, cultural factors such as the quality of educational provision, and many others.

A distinction is sometimes drawn between **simple deprivation**, when a single form of deprivation exists, such as obsolete housing, and **multiple deprivation** when several forms of deprivation exist simultaneously, for example, obsolete housing, high unemployment and high mortality and morbidity rates. The distinction is not a very useful one, because almost all urban deprivation is multiple deprivation. Thus, a simple definition of urban deprivation is difficult, if not impossible, and a good deal of subjectivity is involved in its recognition and delimitation.

According to a report of the Department of the Environment published in 1977, almost 4 million people in the UK lived in 'exceptional concentrations of poverty and deprivation in the declining inner areas of major cities'. Since that date, unemployment in the UK has more than doubled, and the present numbers living in poverty and deprivation are certainly much higher than in 1977. The same 1977 report referred to low-skilled workers in the Stockwell and Brixton districts of Inner London unable to purchase their own homes while at the same time denied access to council housing; it described physical decay and slum housing in the Toxteth district of Inner Liverpool; it noted decayed housing, vandalism, crime and racial tension in the Small Heath district of Inner Birmingham. Four years later, as if to confirm the seriousness of Britain's inner city problems, these same areas figured prominently in the wave of rioting and unrest which swept through Britain's inner cities in 1981 and 1985.

Nor has the situation improved in recent years. In fact, a series of government reports published in the mid-1990s suggested that a growing number of people were caught in the so-called poverty-trap, and drew attention to a growing underclass excluded from the mainstream of society by poverty. For example, a report by the Department of Social Security (1993) suggested that 12 million people were living on incomes less than half the national average, a level that is widely regarded as the unofficial poverty line. The same report suggested that one in four children were living in poverty. Another report noted that in 1979 less than 10% of the population was estimated to be living in poverty, a figure that had risen to 24% in 1990–91. At the same time, reports from the European Commission were noting that the proportion of impoverished households in the UK was the highest in the EU and continuing to increase.

Studies of urban deprivation usually involve the extraction of data from **census returns**. In the UK, the Small Area Statistics compiled by the Office of Population Censuses and Surveys provide a wide range of data for urban areas at enumeration district and ward scale. Information about over-crowding, sub-standard housing and employment structure may be extracted from the Small Area Statistics. Levels of occupancy (room densities) and the sharing of dwellings and facilities provide indices of over-crowding. Sub-standard housing may be revealed by indices which measure the absence of basic facilities, such as hot-water supply, bath and inside WC. Since the census provides no information about personal income, alternative measures must be employed. These include measures of unemployment and low socio-economic status. Low socio-economic status may be expressed by the proportion of unskilled manual workers in the total workforce of an area. A high proportion of such workers earning low wages may indicate poverty or at least financial insecurity.

All the factors mentioned above are **direct indicators** of urban deprivation. In addition, the census also provides data on a number of **indirect indicators** of deprivation. These are factors which may suggest deprivation in an area; for example, a high proportion of pensioner-households or a high proportion of single-parent families. Obviously, not all pensioner-households or single-parent families are deprived, but many are. Similarly, a high proportion of immigrant families may indicate special local needs, although not necessarily so. In other words, the indirect indicators provide supplementary information which may be usefully considered along with the information revealed by the direct indicators.

In 1975, **S. Holtermann** made a study of urban deprivation in Great Britain. She used 18 indicators drawn from the 1971 census, and calculated values for over 87,000 enumeration districts in England, Scotland and Wales. She noted that Clydeside scored as one of the worst areas on almost all indices, while Inner London ranked among the worst cities in terms of housing deprivation. However, in many cases, the results were conflicting. Some areas fared badly on certain criteria, but did relatively well on others. Working in a similar manner, **V. Imber** used ten indicators from the 1971 census which were aggregated to produce a single composite index of deprivation. Clusters of wards with high index values are thus revealed as deprived urban districts.

This paragraph is about problems of identification. In particular it examines the use of indicators of deprivation extracted from the census. The distinction between direct indicators and indirect indicators is made in the next paragraph.

Reference is next made to various studies which have employed census indicators as a means of both identifying and delimiting areas of deprivation in British towns and cities. These include work by Holtermann, Imber and Jarman. There are others that might have been mentioned, but these are sufficient.

In 1984 another index was proposed, by B. Jarman. The **Jarman Index** was originally devised as a method of determining the remuneration of GPs. It sought to recognise the heavier case load of GPs working in impoverished, deprived, urban areas. The index is based on scores for elderly population, single pensioner households, unskilled workers, unemployment, inadequate housing, overcrowding and ethnic minority population. The Jarman index is now widely used to identify areas of urban deprivation.

Although this method of working is attractive in its simplicity, it is not without its limitations and problems. Measurement of deprivation is made difficult by the **lack of information** about essential factors, notably incomes. The choice of indicators extracted from the census is highly **subjective** and greatly affects the resultant scores for an area. An even more serious problem is the lack of **spatial correlation between different indicators**. That is to say, different forms of deprivation appear to exist in different areas. A further problem concerns the fact that levels of deprivation vary within very short distances. For example, in districts which have been subjected to the gentrification process, deprivation and affluence may co-exist side-by-side within small areas. The danger is that **pockets of deprivation** may be hidden by coarse-scale analysis. For example, small areas of deprivation may be obscured by analysis at ward level.

Finally, the whole approach which involves locating deprived **areas** rather than **individuals** has been called into question. It was long assumed that, by identifying deprived urban areas, one would 'catch' most individuals in need. However, that view is now seriously challenged. Work by Holtermann and others has shown that a large proportion of deprived individuals reside outside of those districts which have been selected for special urban improvement programmes, and thus receive no benefit from funds made available for urban renewal. The fact that a growing number of people in Britain are still impoverished and deprived may indicate weaknesses in methods of social research as well as social policy.

Problems and limitations of the methodology are discussed in this paragraph.

The conclusion makes two points. It draws attention to the limitation of area-based policies. Many deprived individuals live outside the areas identified by the methodology described in the essay. It also draws attention to the persistence, and even increase, of areas of deprivation in British cities.

General comments

Questions on topics such as poverty and deprivation, unequal access to resources, and social injustice could appear in a number of different sections of your examination. Inner city problems (housing, homelessness, unemployment, deprivation, crime, etc.) constitute an appropriate theme for inclusion in the section of the exam dealing with urban geography. If your syllabus includes a section on health and welfare, then that could also provide a possible location for questions on poverty and deprivation. It is important to be familiar with your syllabus and to have studied past exam papers as part of your revision.

Related questions

1   Elaborate on the view that urban deprivation in Britain is no longer confined to the inner city.

2   In what ways are the causes and characteristics of deprivation in rural areas different from those of towns and cities?

3   Make a careful definition of each of the following terms: (a) poverty; (b) deprivation; (c) inequality; (d) social injustice. Then, demonstrate ways in which they are interrelated and connected.